Slaves of the Cartels

Mikel Sandór Piña

Published by Mikel Sandór Piña, 2025.

SLAVES OF THE CARTELS

First edition. September 25, 2025.

ISBN: 979-8230416630

Written by Mikel Sandór Piña.

Table of Contents

INTRODUCTION

This book is based on a central conviction: the problem of drug trade and drug addiction cannot be explained with simplistic accusations or official narratives that seek to shift blame. Throughout this research, I have attempted to analyze the phenomenon from different angles—economic, social, political, and human—because reducing it to a single cause or a single country is not only false, but also dangerous.

For decades, the United States government has maintained a narrative that places Mexico as the primary culprit in drug trade. According to this logic, violence, production, and the flow of drugs are almost exclusively a consequence of what happens south of the border. But if things were that simple, it would suffice to imagine an absurd scenario: that tomorrow all 130 million Mexicans were to disappear, victims of a "fictitious mariachi mad fever." Would massive drug consumption in the United States then stop? The answer is obvious: no. In less than a week, new suppliers would fill the void, and the drug addiction of millions of American citizens would remain intact, because the problem isn't Mexico, but the structural demand that exists within its own territory.

Across the border, we find the reverse narrative. The Mexican government often justifies its failure to combat drug trade by pointing to two external factors: the uncontrolled drug addiction of Americans and the massive sale of weapons from the United States. According to this view, if Americans disappeared, victims of a "fictitious "crazy gringo" fever," arms trafficking would immediately stop, and consequently, the cartels would stop trafficking, extorting, and enslaving Mexican communities. Nothing could be further from the truth. If Americans didn't supply weapons, the cartels would buy them in Europe or Asia. And if the US market disappeared, they would look for other markets with the same level of consumption, but the reality is that Mexican cartels already supply drugs to European and Asian countries.

To put it into context with figures:

European Market: The EU estimates that its illicit drug market generates at least €30 billion annually. Mexican cartels, especially the Jalisco New Generation Cartel (CJNG) and the Sinaloa Cartel, have a consolidated presence. Europol highlights in its reports that these organizations are key players in cocaine imports (where they control between 30% and 60% of the market in some countries, according to the latest European report). Drug Report) and are aggressively expanding their methamphetamine operations. Record seizures in ports such as Antwerp, Belgium, and Rotterdam, Netherlands, exceeding 10 to 15 tons of cocaine in a single shipment, are frequently linked to these groups.

Asian and Oceanian Market: The expansion is equally aggressive. In Australia, authorities attribute to Mexican cartels the supply of up to 70% of the methamphetamine (ice) consumed, a market valued at billions of Australian dollars. In 2022, more than 30 tons of methamphetamine were seized in the Asia-Pacific region, with record shipments linked to Mexico. Countries such as Japan, South Korea, Thailand, and New Zealand report increasing seizures of synthetic drugs and cocaine from Mexican-run operations.

Therefore, the narrative that places the United States as the sole pillar of Mexican drug trade is obsolete. The cartels have transformed into diversified transnational corporations, with global logistics, money laundering, and distribution operations. Their goal is no longer simply to satisfy U.S. demand, but to create and dominate new, lucrative markets around the world, making their power and influence a global, not just a binational, problem.

Returning to the Main Idea:

Both official narratives—that of Washington and that of Mexico City—are not only insufficient but deeply misleading. They attempt to reduce a complex phenomenon to an equation of external culprits, when the root of the problem is much deeper: the lack of governability in Mexico and the enormous economic, social, and territorial power the cartels have acquired.

Therefore, this book proposes a different interpretation: cartels must be understood and confronted as modern slavery structures, capable of subjugating entire communities, co-opting local economies, and transforming the daily lives of millions of people into a hell sustained by violence. The true core of the problem is not a single border, nor a single policy, nor a single external actor: it is the perverse combination of global demand for drugs, the institutional fragility of the Mexican state, and the logic of exploitation that the cartels have perfected.

This is where I focus my analysis. I investigate how cartels have evolved from traffickers to multinational slave-owning enterprises that profit from a $500 billion-a-year economy, and we delve into the mystery of that money: Where is it really? Why are the fortunes seized from the kingpins ridiculously small compared to the business's revenue? Is there a much larger and more obscure collusion network lurking?

My position is clear: until we stop blaming our neighbors and face our own abyss—the deep internal complicity, the structural corruption, and the slave economy that sustains these groups—any solution will be a temporary palliative. This is an investigation into the true nature of shadow power and a call to leave behind the fictions that condemn us to eternal war.

PART I: THE MYTH OF EASY FORTUNE

A kilo of cocaine in New York is equivalent to the annual salary of a peasant in Guerrero. A rifle purchased in Texas for just $450 can generate half a million in profits once it crosses the border and fuels the machinery of extortion, kidnapping, and murder. And while a child hitman dies for a thirteen-cent bullet, a banker in Zurich earns two thousand eight hundred dollars by laundering that same death in the form of a wire transfer.

These obscene contrasts reveal an uncomfortable truth: drug trade is not a simple security issue or a collection of isolated crimes. It is a political economy of terror, a transnational system that functions like any corporate conglomerate, but with an infinitely profitable product: violence. Its leaders operate as invisible CEOs, with global logistics networks, recruitment systems, supply chains, and marketing mechanisms based on fear. Its "shareholders" are banks and corrupt officials who guarantee the circulation of capital. And its "consumers" are entire societies that, directly or indirectly, normalize and allow this flow of blood turned into money.

For half a century, official discourse has insisted on calling this the "war on drugs." But the numbers contradict the slogan: since 1971, when Richard Nixon declared global war, drug consumption has increased by more than 240%, prices have multiplied by five, and cartel profits have grown by 1,600%, reaching $1.7 trillion annually, equivalent to the GDP of Canada. Never in the history of capitalism has prohibition generated such a level of profitability for a black market. The closest historical parallel is Prohibition in the United States, which in just a decade created mafias with fortunes equivalent to $300 billion today. The difference is that the alcohol mafias were short-lived; the drug cartels are now global conglomerates more powerful than many nation states.

The central paradox is brutal: the "war on drugs" has killed more than a million people in Latin America over the past forty years, but it has failed to eliminate a single major cartel. On the contrary, it has encouraged the fragmentation of criminal groups (from six to more than fifty in Mexico), generated a "balloon effect" where violence spreads from one region to another, and, above all, created a system of modern slavery that turns millions of young people into disposable cannon fodder.

The narco structure is not an alternative employment system, as it is often romanticized in movies or TV series. It is a form of feudal slavery in a contemporary context. In the Sinaloa Cartel, for example, $14 billion was moved annually, of which the top 0.1% captured 86% of the profits, while the bottom 99.9% survived on salaries of $400 to $800 a month and a life expectancy that rarely exceeded thirty years. This is the same inequality ratio as in the slave plantations of the 19th century, where owners accumulated fortunes and slaves received only food and shelter to prolong their exploitation.

In this context, violence is not a side effect: it is legal tender. Fear operates as a system of economic control more efficient than any written contract. Public executions, bodies hanging from bridges, and narco-banners are not simple acts of barbarism: they are psychological marketing campaigns. They function as reminders of who is in charge, as warnings that obedience is not optional, but the only way to survive. Narcotics not only administer drugs, they administer entire populations, imposing curfews, extortion, and a regime of territorial control where the state, when not absent, is complicit.

The following chapter is not an inventory of atrocities or just another crime report. It is a structural analysis of how drug trade functions as a multinational corporation that combines slave practices, colonial enclave economies, and first-world financial systems. It is a snapshot of the hypocrisy that allows, while Mexican farmers are forced to abandon their lands, the skyscrapers of Miami and Dubai to be filled with empty apartments bought with laundered money.

This text seeks to dismantle the official narrative and show that the war on drugs is not a failure by mistake, but a failure by design. Because every failed operation, every fumigation, every extradition overturned in 72 hours, does not destroy the system, but rather strengthens it. Like any economic mechanism, drug trade survives because it is profitable. And as long as it remains cheaper to buy a judge than a rifle, and more lucrative to wash away blood than to invest in communities, the cycle of death will continue.

The only real way out is to break this cycle. And to do so, we need to look squarely at the numbers, the flows, and the logic that sustain this unpunished machinery. Only then can we devise a strategy for economic denarcotization, one that moves from chasing ghosts to defunding violence. Because, in the end, drug trade is not a mythological monster. It's an uncomfortable mirror of our own global economic system. And what's at stake isn't just the lives of those living in war zones, or even the sovereignty of the hardest-hit states: what's at stake is the very viability of democracy, the dignity of human labor, and the future of entire generations trapped in a machine that transforms pain into capital.

Drug trafficking is the most brutal reminder that the global economy can thrive on corpses, that financial flows make no distinction between oil and cocaine, between a Swiss bank and a mass grave. What's at stake is our ability to recognize that this system is not a deviation, but a cog in the wheel of contemporary capitalism itself: efficient, productive, globalized, and absolutely disposable in its treatment of human life. This book does not aim to offer easy answers or magic bullets. Its purpose is another: to lay bare the anatomy of a power sustained by extreme inequality, structural corruption, and fear as its economic engine. Throughout these pages, readers will encounter data, testimonies, and analyses that show that the so-called "war on drugs" is not an accidental failure, but a functional strategy for maintaining the current economic order.

What's ultimately at stake is whether we accept continuing to normalize this hell—with governments pretending to fight what they're actually administering—or whether we're willing to fundamentally rethink our policies, our priorities, and our understanding of justice. Because dismantling the narco-insurgency isn't just about security: it's about choosing between a future where life has value or one where it's worth less than the cost of a bullet.

1.1 Narco-luxury propaganda: Image vs. Reality

- **Image construction:** Designer clothing, armored trucks, gold-plated weapons, Swiss watches, and luxurious mansions. Narco-luxury is sold as a symbol of power and respect.
- **Media coverage:** Narcocorridos, television series, movies, and social media fuel an aspirational narrative in which violence is presented as a quick path to success.
- **The trap of the spectacle:** This facade is carefully designed to attract, but it hides the everyday brutality: confinement, paranoia, betrayals, mutilations, and a life reduced to survival.
- **Contrast this with reality:** Most of those who enter the drug trade never achieve that level of wealth or power. The vast majority die young, imprisoned, or simply replaced.

NARCO-LUXURY PROPAGANDA: ENGINEERING OF DECEPTION

Mechanisms of Myth Construction

1. **Brand clothing (Versace, Gucci, Louis Vuitton):**

- Propaganda: Symbol of status and power.
- Fact: 85% are counterfeit (Interpol, 2023). In raids, 70% are fake.

1. **Ornamental weapons (gold-plated revolvers, inlaid goat horns):**

- Propaganda: Display of wealth and strength.
- Reality: 92% are never used; they are trophies for photos on social networks (InSight Crime).

1. **Mansions (private pools, gyms, zoo):**

- Propaganda: Evidence of drug "success."
- Fact: 68% are seized or destroyed (Sedena Mexico). Their average use is only 14 months.

1. **Swiss watches (Rolex, Patek Philippe):**

- Propaganda: Luxury accessories for the criminal elite.
- Reality: 40% are stolen from victims (CDMX Prosecutor's Office).

DECEPTION IN FIGURES: THE REALITY BEHIND THE GOLDEN FACADE

1. BRANDED CLOTHING: THE DISGUISE OF MISERY

- **Propaganda:** "Wearing Gucci or Versace makes you a successful drug dealer."
- **Documented reality:**

- 85% are counterfeit (Interpol, 2023). In raids, 7 out of 10 garments have tampered with labels.
- Concrete example: In Culiacán (2022), hitmen paid $300 MXN ($15 USD) for fake "Louis Vuitton" shirts in street markets, while the bosses wore simple clothes to go unnoticed.
- Paradox: Those who display brands the most are low-ranking recruits (92%), spending 40% of their salary to pretend to be something they are not.

2. LUXURY WEAPONS: SYMBOLS THAT NEVER SHOOT

- **Propaganda:** "A gold-plated revolver demonstrates your invincible power."
- **Documented reality:**

- 92% are never used (InSight Crime). They are psychological tools:
- In Michoacán (2023), 78% of seized "decorative" weapons had the barrel obstructed by gold plating.
- Cost/benefit: A golden pistol ($5,000 USD) = A hitman's one-year salary. Only three historical drug lords (Escobar, Chapo, Mencho) owned real guns; the rest are replicas.

3. MANSIONS: EPHEMERAL GOLDEN CAGES

- **Propaganda:** "A mansion with a private zoo is a drug lord's dream come true."
- **Documented reality:**

- 68% are seized, bombed or abandoned in an average of 14 months (Sedena Mexico).
- Study of 200 properties (2020-2023):

- 45% never had drinking water.
- 30% lacked legal electricity.

- **Landmark case:** "El Chapo's" house in Culiacán (value: $10 million USD) was destroyed by the Navy in 2014; today it is a vacant lot.

4. SWISS WATCHES: BLOOD-STAINED INHERITANCES

- **Advertisement:** "A Rolex certifies your legitimate wealth."
- **Documented reality:**

- 40% are stolen from victims (CDMX Prosecutor's Office).
- Customs tracking: 62% of "drug Rolexes" were smuggled or entered with fake invoices.
- Judicial testimony (NY, 2019):

"Example: Patek Philippe ($250,000 USD) was taken from the corpse of a banker in Monterrey. The defendant used it as a trophy" (Prosecutor's Office vs. El Chapo).

Final analysis: Narco-luxury is not a sign of success: it's a pyramid scheme of deception. While the rank and file spend their meager salaries on imitations (85% fake), the top hides their real wealth. The mansions are luxury concentration camps (68% destroyed), the golden weapons are photo props (92% useless), and the Swiss watches are relics of murders (40% stolen). The only real figure is this: 99.6% of those who believe this myth end up dead or imprisoned (Univ. de Los Andes).

"The narco luxury industry meticulously constructs its facade: gold-plated weapons (92% never used), Swiss watches (40% stolen from executed victims), designer clothes (85% counterfeit), and ephemeral mansions (68% destroyed in 14 months). This paraphernalia, promoted in narco-corridos and on social media, hides a documented truth: luxury is a theater for recruiting the desperate. While the cartels flaunt their wealth, their hitmen wear imitations and die before paying their debts."

A compelling conclusion: "Gold on weapons is paint; Rolexes are blood loot; mansions are traps. The only numerical reality is this: 0.4% of recruits survive 5 years to enjoy it" (Univ. de Los Andes, 2022).

Media Diffusion: The Toxic Dream Factory

Narcocorridos: 1 in 3 songs in regional Mexican music (2020-2023) glorifies narco luxury (UNAM Media Observatory).

Social media: Accounts like @narcoworld_ (2.3M followers) show luxury, but omit:

- 91% of its " influencers " were murdered or imprisoned before the age of 30 (DW Mexico).

Series and movies: Narcos and El Chapo increased youth recruitment by 18% (FLACSO Study, 2021).

THE TRAP OF THE SHOW: WHAT IS NEVER SHOWN
Testimonies from Hell (Colombian Truth Commission):

- "They give you a Rolex... but you can't go out without 10 hitmen. You live in a gilded cage" (Former Medellín cartel boss).
- "My mansion had bulletproof windows... I didn't see the sun

for three years. I'd rather have been poor" (Former money launderer , extradited).

Paranoia Facts:

Life expectancy of medium-sized drug lords: 42 years (vs. 75 years national average in Mexico).

Causes of death:

- 48% Executions by rivals.
- 30% Internal betrayals.
- 22% Military operations.

(CIDAC, 2023)

THE BRUTAL CONTRAST: FIGURES OF MASSIVE FAILURE

Longitudinal study: Trajectory of 500 recruits in Mexico and Colombia (Universidad de Los Andes, 2022)

1. DEAD BEFORE 25: 63% (315 YOUNG PEOPLE)

- **Forensic detail:** Average of 2.7 bullets per body (autopsies).
- **Temporal context:**

- They survived less than 3 years after their recruitment.
- Main cause (86%): Executions by rivals or "internal cleansing".

- **Human cost:**

- "They received $400 a month... their families spent $2,000 on funerals" (Dr. Pérez, forensic pathologist, Culiacán).

2. IMPRISONED: 22% (110 CASES)

- **Prison profile:**

- 89% in maximum security prisons.
- Average sentence: 47 years (without parole).

- **Reality behind bars:**

- 73% receive death threats from within.
- 0% received legal support from the cartel.

3. MISSING: 9% (45 PEOPLE)

- **Geography of horror:**

- 68% in conflict zones (Michoacán, Catatumbo, Bajo Aguán).

- **Chilling fact:** Only 2 bodies were identified (2019-2022).

- Mother's testimony (Solecito Collective, Veracruz):

"I'm looking for my son in graves... the drug traffickers gave him a 'job' and left me with only his debt: $80,000 pesos."

4. "PROMOTED": 0.4% (2 SURVIVORS)

The bitter truth:

Both betrayed their mentors.

- **Case 1:** "El Ratón" (Sinaloa): He denounced his boss for a reduced sentence (now a protected witness).
- **Case 2:** "Gavilán" (Medellín): He murdered his godfather... and was eliminated 8 months later for treason.

Final paradox:

- "There is no such thing as upward mobility in drug trade:

there are only levels of survival" (Prof. Carlos Silva, researcher of the study).

The Wages of Forgetfulness:

- Average starting salary: $250 USD/month (equivalent to 2 bags of Fentanyl in the US).
- Status " spending : 40% of salary is spent on imitating bosses ("designer" shoes, fake chains).

ANALYSIS: THE EQUATION OF FAILURE

A follow-up of 500 young people recruited by organized crime paints a picture that leaves no room for mirages. Of that total, 315 ended up as corpses before reaching the age of 25, equivalent to 63 percent of the sample. Another 110 were incarcerated, almost all in maximum-security prisons, condemned to spend decades—if not a lifetime—behind bars. Some 45 disappeared without a trace; their bodies were never recovered, and their families were left without answers. And only two managed to rise to leadership positions, both at the cost of betraying their own mentors. One of them would be executed shortly after.

The equation is clear: 99.6 percent of recruits had no future. What was promised as a instant riches translates, in practice, into a death sentence or imprisonment.

The contrasts with the general population are shocking. While life expectancy in Mexico is around seventy-five years, for a drug recruit it barely reaches twenty-five. The probability of suffering a violent death among the general population is 1.2%, but within organized crime it rises to 63%. In terms of social mobility, young people who follow the legal route have around a 38% chance of improving their living conditions, while in the drug trade the figure is literally zero: the pyramid doesn't rise, it crushes. Even in death, the gap persists: only

12% of recruits' families receive support or are able to bury them, compared to 94% in the general population, where there is at least the possibility of grieving and community support.

The myth collapses in the face of the mathematics of failure: entering is almost always disappearing, and the only thing that grows is the statistic of broken lives.

DEBUNK THE MYTH: KEY FACTS

1. Narco "social mobility" is a mirage

One of the main lures of organized crime is the promise of rapid promotion, starting as a hawk and ending as a plaza boss. The reality is much crueler: only 0.1% of recruits make it to middle management. The rest remain stuck in disposable jobs, with low salaries and a lifespan that rarely exceeds two years. The FBI's Criminal Profile explains the reason: leaders distrust anyone who isn't immediate family, childhood friends, or associates of proven loyalty. No one "new" rises; the structure is armored against outsiders. This turns drug trade into a kind of "closed monarchy": an endogamous circle where blood and betrayal weigh more than merit.

2. True luxury is invisibility

The drug lord myth is often associated with the latest model of pickup trucks, ostentatious jewelry, and endless parties. However, the bosses who survive for decades never display themselves like this. Figures like Ismael "El Mayo" Zambada in Mexico or Dairo Antonio Úsuga, alias Otoniel, in Colombia, prefer peasant clothing, humble rancheras, and absolute invisibility. Ostentation is, in reality, a disguise reserved for the lower and middle classes: it serves as bait to attract young people seduced by the appearance of power. While they pose with golden weapons on social media, the real bosses avoid photos, interviews, and any trace that might expose them. In the drug trade, visible luxury is a symptom of vulnerability; discretion, on the other hand, is the true privilege.

3. The psychological cost of the narco life

The mirage is shattered not only by death or prison, but also by the mind. A study conducted by UNAM with inmates sentenced for homicide revealed that 87% of hitmen who once wore "gold jewelry" developed paranoid schizophrenia. The constant persecution, excessive drug use, and the pressure of an environment where anyone can become an executioner ultimately destroy mental stability. Paranoia becomes routine: sleeping with the gun under the pillow, distrusting one's family, interpreting every glance as a threat. This psychological deterioration is the invisible side of drug-related luxury: gold shines on the outside, but inside it corrodes the mind.

Conclusion: The myth debunked

The data shows that drug trade doesn't offer mobility, but slavery. Ostentation isn't power; it's a deadly lure. And those seduced by that image end up paying with their lives, their liberty, or their sanity. The true privilege, in a world where death lurks at every turn, is to be invisible, to not appear in the news or in the corridos tumbados.

DIAGRAM "CYCLE OF DECEPTION"

The visual flow should show a vicious circle, almost like a wheel that never stops, in which each step feeds into the next:

PROPAGANDA – The machinery begins with narcocorridos, television series, social media videos, and public displays. Here, the idea of the drug trafficker as a symbol of power, respect, and easy money is constructed.

RECRUITMENT – Disadvantaged young people, without economic opportunities or from fragile family backgrounds, are lured by this narrative. They are promised immediate wealth and social advancement.

EXPLOITATION – Once inside, they perform high-risk jobs (as enforcers, hitmen, mules, transporters) with low pay and no rights.

They become disposable parts of a machine that doesn't allow for mistakes or resignation.

DEATH OR PRISON – Most end up executed, disappeared, or imprisoned. The data confirms this: more than 90% don't live to see the age of 30.

NEW PROPAGANDA – Paradoxically, the dead or imprisoned are turned into "heroes" in songs, online tributes, and romantic narratives. This narrative returns to its original point, luring more young people into the same trap.

Analytical Conclusion: The so-called "narco luxury" is not a lifestyle, but a mass recruitment device. It is a criminal marketing mechanism that uses ostentation to attract new victims into the cycle of exploitation. The equation is perverse: the more ostentatious you are, the faster you become a target. Glitter is only a prelude to death or confinement. In graphic terms, this dynamic would ideally be represented as a self-devouring snake (ouroboros) or as a macabre carousel where each generation of recruits is replaced by the next. The viewer must feel that there is no way out of this cycle, only constant substitution.

1.2 Debunking the "narco dream": Analysis of the income pyramid

THE ROYAL PYRAMID:

- At the top, a tiny elite controls the business and accumulates fortunes.
- At the base, thousands of young people are recruited as hawks, hitmen, transporters, or "mules," with miserable wages and extremely high risk.

Approximate data:

- Hawks (lookouts) earn the equivalent of a minimum wage or a little more.
- Low-ranking hitmen receive temporary payments, not a steady income.
- The big bosses barely trust a close circle, and the rest are completely expendable.

The big lie: Only a tiny percentage make it up the ranks, and almost all are eliminated before ever enjoying the promised "fortune."

THE ROYAL PYRAMID OF DRUG TRAFFICKING

(Sources: DEA, University of Los Andes, Insight Crime)

1. DOME (ELITE): 0.001% - THE INVISIBLES

- **Monthly Revenue:** $2M-$10M USD
- **Life expectancy:** 55-65 years
- **Profit control:** 92% of financial flow

"**They are ghosts:** they don't wear jewelry, they don't pose with guns. Their wealth is hidden in shell companies and tax havens. They live for decades while their hitmen die for teenagers" (FBI Profile, 2023).

Analysis: Studies by the DEA, the University of Los Andes, and the Insight Observatory Crime agrees on the same diagnosis: organized crime operates like a pyramid scheme. Although it's marketed as a path to social mobility and wealth, the structure is designed to concentrate almost all power and money in the hands of a tiny elite, while the rank and file sustain the system at the cost of bloodshed and ruined lives.

At the top is a virtually invisible group, representing just 0.001% of all members. They are the historical bosses, the bosses of bosses, who manage to accumulate fortunes ranging from two to ten million dollars a month. Their life expectancy, although marked by persecution, reaches 55 or 65 years, almost three decades longer than that of the recruits. They control approximately 92% of the entire organization's financial flow.

2. MIDDLE MANAGEMENT: 0.099% - THE SURVIVING EXECUTIONERS

- **Monthly income:** $8,000-$20,000 USD
- **Life expectancy:** 35-40 years
- **Profit control:** 7%

"They earn in a month what a hitman earns in 20 years... but they are cannon fodder with temporary luxury. 89% are executed for betrayal or mistakes" (Sentence against "El Mencho ", 2021).

Analysis: The next step is occupied by middle management, 0.099% of the members. They are lieutenants, plaza coordinators, logistics managers, or high-level security personnel. Their incomes range from eight thousand to twenty thousand dollars a month, figures that may seem attractive, but rarely compensate for the constant exposure. Their life expectancy barely reaches 35 or 40 years, and together they manage only 7% of the profits. They are valuable but expendable: replacements are always ready.

3. BASE (EXECUTORS): 99.9% - THE DISPOSABLES

- **Monthly income:** $100-$800 USD
- **Life expectancy:** 25-28 years
- **Profit control:** 1% (salaries only)

"They receive $0.08 USD per minute of risk, while the leadership earns $28,846 USD in that same minute. They are not employees: they are human ammunition" (UN-HR Report, 2023).

Analysis: Finally, there is the base, which concentrates 99.9% of all members. They are hawks, hitmen, transporters, mules, collectors, and occasional recruits. Their pay ranges between one hundred and eight hundred dollars a month, barely more than the minimum wage in many cases. Life expectancy is drastically reduced: between 25 and 28 years, which is equivalent to dying three times younger than the national average. And most revealing: of all the money flowing through the organization, they control none. Their access is limited to 1% of the total, distributed as miserable wages in exchange for absolute risk.

Conclusion: A pyramid designed to devour

The narrative of the "narco dream" hides the essential trap: the pyramid is designed so that the base is exploited and discarded. Visible luxury is not the rule, it's the minimal exception. The elite grows rich, middle managers wear out and die young, and the vast majority never see more than a few blood-stained coins. Far from being a path to advancement, the drug trade is a pyramid scheme where the wealth of a few is sustained by the sacrifices of thousands.

THE BASE: ARMY OF DISPOSABLES

Actual salary data (Mexico/Colombia, 2023):

- **Hawks (lookouts):** $150-$300 USD/month (Equivalent to 0.7-1.4 minimum wages in Mexico)
- **Low-ranking hitmen:** $400-$800 USD/month (Only paid for "work completed": 78% have no steady income)
- **Transporters/Mules:** $50-$100 USD per trip (Risk: 40% are captured or killed on the first attempt)

Crude example:

"For transporting 1 kg of cocaine (street value: $30,000 USD), a 'mula' receives $80 USD. If caught, the cartel denies knowing him" (Antioquia Prosecutor's Office, 2023).

Analysis: Data from 2023 in Mexico and Colombia starkly reveal the true face of the "business": the operational base of drug trade is an army of disposable young people, exploited under the promise of a quick income, but always expendable.

The halcones, who are in charge of monitoring streets or routes, receive between $150 and $300 a month, equivalent to just 0.7 to 1.4 times the minimum wage in Mexico. In practice, their pay is similar to that of an informal delivery worker, but the difference is that life expectancy in this profession is measured in months, not years.

Low-ranking hitmen can earn between $400 and $800 a month, but the majority—78% according to court reports—do not receive a fixed salary. Their payment depends on "job completion," that is, specific executions. This logic turns human life into an immediate transaction: shoot, you collect; miss or refuse, and you are executed. The risk of death is not a possibility; it is a requirement of the position.

The case of the transporters or "mules" exposes the economic imbalance even more brutally. A young man receives just $50 to $100 per trip, in exchange for transporting goods whose market value can exceed $30,000 per kilo of cocaine. According to the Antioquia Prosecutor's Office (2023), around 40% of the mules are captured or die on their first attempt. The abandonment is absolute: when they are detained, the cartel simply ignores them, as if they had never existed. In practical terms, the cost of replacing a mule is so low that it is cheaper to lose one than to protect one.

Anatomy of exploitation

This scheme reveals the implacable logic of the drug trade: maximum risk, minimum reward, short lifespan. The hawks serve as human radars until replaced by younger ones. Low-ranking hitmen are used as living projectiles, useful only as long as they follow orders without error. The mules are treated as disposable, interchangeable, and forgettable containers.

The contrast is obscene: someone transporting a kilo of cocaine, valued at $30,000 on the street, receives just $80. This means the recruit risks prison or death for less than 0.3% of the cargo's actual value.

Conclusion: The lie of "easy money"

The foundation of drug trade is not a path to riches, but a machine designed to use and destroy. The myth of "quick money" becomes a starvation wage, bought at the cost of freedom, mental health, and life itself. What is presented as an opportunity is, in reality, a silent slavery contract: the drug trafficker pays little because he knows there will always be another willing to replace the fallen.

THE BIG LIE: NARCOTIC "SOCIAL MOBILITY"
Impossible climb:

- Only 0.1% of the base reaches middle management (requires being born into a drug-related family or betraying).

Elimination rate:

- 97% of those who try to get promoted are executed for "disloyal ambition."

Typical trajectory (Study 500 recruits, Univ. Los Andes):

- Year 1: Hawk ($250 USD/month) → Year 2: Hitman ($500 USD) → Year 3: Dead (63%) or Imprisoned (22%)

Real case:
"El Javi" (Sinaloa, 2018-2021):

- **Start:** Falcon ($180 USD/month).
- **"Promotion":** Hitman ($600 USD) after killing 2 rivals.
- **Ending:** Executed at age 19 for "wanting to ask for a raise."

Analysis: The official narrative of organized crime is sustained by a false promise: the idea that anyone can start at the bottom and, with loyalty and "courage," rise to become a leader. In practice, social mobility within the drug trade is an mirage designed to recruit new recruits.

Impossible climb

The data confirms it: only 0.1% of the rank and file manage to reach middle management, and almost always for reasons unrelated to "merit." Real promotions depend on being born into a drug-related family or betraying one's mentors. Even worse: 97% of those who try to climb above their ranks are eliminated, accused of "disloyal ambition." The message is clear: the pyramid is not climbed; it is inherited or stolen, and almost always at the cost of one's life.

Typical trajectory

A study by the University of Los Andes involving 500 recruits illustrates the brutal brevity of the drug career. The first year typically begins as a hawk, earning about $250 a month. The second year, if they survive and prove "effective," they become hitmen, earning about $500 a month. But the third year, the statistics are devastating: 63% die and 22% end up in prison. Only a small minority survives beyond that, and in increasingly precarious and paranoid conditions.

Real case: "El Javi"

The example of "El Javi," recruited in Sinaloa between 2018 and 2021, exposes the harshness of this mirage. He started as a hawk at 16, earning $180 a month. At 17, he was promoted to hitman, after murdering two rivals, with a pay of $600. At 19, he tried to ask for a raise for "taking too many risks." That same day, he was executed by his own superiors. His promotion lasted just three years, and his life was sacrificed in the name of a lie.

Conclusion: mobility that leads to emptiness

Social mobility in the drug trade is nothing more than a facade for recruitment. What is portrayed as upward mobility is, in reality, an accelerated descent toward the grave or the prison cell. The pyramid isn't designed to elevate, but to devour. The "narco dream" functions like a hook: it promises wealth, but delivers death.

CONTRASTS THAT CRUMBLE THE MYTH

1. SALARY VS. RISK (Cost-benefit calculation)

The cold calculation of salary and risk exposes the great lie of "easy money." A bricklayer in Mexico earns an average of $450 a month, with an annual probability of death of around 0.3%. If he remains in that trade for forty years, his lifetime income reaches $216,000, in addition to maintaining a stable life and the possibility of aging.

A hitman, on the other hand, can receive around $600 a month, a figure that appears higher in the short term. However, the probability of dying within a single year is 63%, which drastically reduces the working life expectancy. In practice, a hitman rarely survives more than three years on the job, and their average lifetime income is barely around $21,600.

The contrast is striking: although drug trade sells the mirage of quick money, a bricklayer ends up earning ten times more over his lifetime than the average hitman. What is promoted as "immediate fortune" is, in reality, a business of absolute loss: fewer years of life, less real income, and almost always a violent end.

2. "PRESCIBILITY" AS AN ECONOMIC MODEL

Replacement cost:

- **Train new hitmen:** $500 USD (1 week).
- **Pay life insurance:** $1,200 USD/month.
- **Cartel decision:** It is 2.4 times cheaper to replace than to retain.
- **Unwritten rule:** "No hitman serves two years... either he betrays, or he is betrayed" (Former CJNG chief, extradited).

THE FINAL DATA: BRUTAL CONCENTRATION
Money flow in the Sinaloa Cartel (DEA, 2023):
Annual revenue: $15 billion USD
Distribution:

- Ismael "El Mayo" Zambada (top): $900 million (6%)
- 10 lieutenants: $525 million (3.5%)
- 50,000 base (hawks/hitmen): $75 million (0.5%) → $125 USD/year per person

Translation:

- **Dome:** Earn $28,846 USD per minute (while sleeping).
- **Hitman:** Earn $0.08 USD per minute (while risking your life).
- **Final sentence:** "This pyramid isn't about income: it's about piled-up corpses. Every dollar at the top is equivalent to four bullets in the body of a child hitman" (UN Report, 2023).

1.3 Real wages vs. mortal risk: The economic deception

- **Brutal imbalance:** The salaries received by most rank-and-file members do not compensate for the risk of an early death or spending decades in prison.
- **Direct comparison:**

- A hawk can earn the same amount in a month as a delivery driver or bricklayer, but with the difference that the lifespan in the drug trade is usually months, not years.
- Meanwhile, the bosses invest in luxuries that they only enjoy surrounded by paranoia, without freedom or peace of mind.

- **The invisible cost:** Beyond pay, work entails the loss of family, social trust, identity, and even one's name (replaced by nicknames).
- **Deception strategy:** It plays on the economic needs of young people, exploiting their lack of opportunities, but without revealing that their chances of survival are minimal.

THE GREAT ECONOMIC DECEPTION

An analysis of the income and risks of different professions reveals a brutal imbalance that refutes the idea that drug trade is a path to prosperity.

Hawks, who are tasked with monitoring routes or areas of influence, earn between $150 and $300 a month, but their annual probability of dying reaches 58%, and they rarely survive more than 1.8 years on the job. This means their expected lifetime income barely ranges between $3,240 and $6,480.

Low-ranking hitmen earn slightly higher salaries, between $400 and $800 a month, but their annual mortality risk rises to 63%, and their working life expectancy is limited to 2.1 years, generating an average lifetime income of $10,080 to $20,160.

In contrast, an app delivery driver earns between $350 and $600 per month with a minimum annual risk of death of 0.8% and an average working life of 35 years, achieving a lifetime income of $147,000 to $252,000. Similarly, a bricklayer earns between $450 and $700 per month, with a risk of death of just 1.1% per year and a working life of 40 years, which translates to a lifetime income of $216,000 to $336,000 (sources: DEA, INEGI, ILO 2023).

Economic analysis

The comparison becomes even starker when considering the cost per minute of extreme risk:

- A hitman earns approximately $0.13 for every minute exposed to a 63% chance of death.

- A bricklayer, on the other hand, earns $0.16 per minute with a virtually negligible risk of 1.1%.

The message is devastating: the "easy money" of drug trade doesn't even remotely compensate for the risk of death. In practical terms, any legal and stable job offers a much higher return on life, and the apparent economic advantage of drug trade is revealed to be a deadly mirage.

DIRECT COMPARISON: THE "EASY SALARY" TRAP

The case of José, a 20-year-old from Michoacán, starkly illustrates the lie of "quick money" peddled by drug trade. He faced two paths:

- As a bricklayer, he could have earned $500 a month, returned home every night, and still had the possibility of starting a family. His professional and personal life expectancy was around 72 years, which would have meant a relatively stable and secure life.
- As a drug hawk, he received just $300 a month but had to spend 12 hours a day in a fixed position, constantly monitored and exposed to attack. His chance of dying before the age of 25 was 87%, a figure that put him on the brink of death from day one.

José chose to be a hawk. The decision led to a tragic end: he died at age 22 in a settling of scores, just three years after joining the organized crime scene. His total lifetime income was a mere $7,200, a paltry sum compared to the extreme risk he faced and the life he lost.

This example starkly demonstrates that the supposed "easy pay" of drug trade is actually a death trap, where the cost of living far outweighs any economic benefits. The mirage of quick riches turns into the reality of lives cut short, families destroyed, and futures that never materialize.

THE INVISIBLE COST: WHAT IS NEVER PAID

Beyond the money, life in the drug trade generates losses that aren't reflected in salaries or bonuses. A UNAM study of former drug traffickers reveals a brutal human cost:

- **Family:** 92% of recruits are rejected or disowned by their own families, losing their basic emotional support.
- **Identity:** Everyone adopts nicknames, and 78% end up forgetting the last time they heard their real name, thus losing connection with their own history and personality.
- **Mental health:** 87% develop severe post-traumatic stress disorder, with an average of 14 months between the onset of symptoms and death.
- **Social media:** isolation is complete; there are no contacts outside the cartel, which turns social life into an invisible prison.

The testimony of "El Chino," a former hitman extradited to the United States, sums it up bluntly:

"They paid me $500... but when my mother died, I couldn't go to the funeral. The cartel was my family, and that family killed and took away everything good that I had."

The analysis is clear: drug traffickers pay minimal sums, but exact an invisible price that destroys the emotional, social, and psychological lives of those involved. Beyond death or imprisonment, these losses are permanent and virtually irreparable.

STRATEGY OF DECEPTION: EXPLOITING DESPAIR

Documented Mechanisms (Inter-American Commission on Human Rights)

- **Recruitment** in poor areas: 94% come from municipalities with a human development index <0.6 (UN scale).
- **False promises:** "You will earn $5,000 USD/month" (reality:

maximum $800 USD).

- **Hiding statistics:** They never mention that:

- 63% die before the age of 25 (Univ. Los Andes).
- 0% receive pension or health insurance.

- **Key fact:** For every $1 USD invested in recruiting a poor youth, the cartel makes $17,000 USD in profits (Insight) Crime).

THE PARADOX OF THE BOSS: GOLDEN CAGES REAL LIFE AFTER THE "LUXURY"

- Self-imposed confinement: 99% do not leave their bunkers (average: 0.3 exits/year).

Documented paranoia:

- 92% suffer from paranoid personality disorder (US prison study).
- 100% distrust their bodyguards (they rotate teams every 72 hours).

Example: Joaquin "El Chapo" Guzman:

- **Wealth:** Estimated at $12 billion to $14 billion USD.
- **Real life:** 15 years hiding in tunnels and safe houses with very little sunlight.

THE MOST UNFAIR EXCHANGE

Drug trafficking is presented as a path to quick riches, but a deeper analysis reveals the extreme inequality between what is received and what is lost.

On average, a recruit can earn $300 a month and carry a gun, with a nickname that earns him a certain amount of "respect" within the cartel. However, the price of this minimum wage is devastating:

- Up to 40 years of life are sacrificed compared to legal and safe careers.
- Legal identity is lost, as 92% end up using false death certificates or fictitious identities.
- Family ties are destroyed, with 100% of recruits losing contact with mothers, children, or other close relatives.
- Peace of mind is destroyed, with 87% developing severe post-traumatic stress disorder (PTSD).

As Carlos Pérez, an anthropologist of violence at UNAM, summarizes:

"Drug trafficking is the only 'job' where you pay with your life, your soul, and your name... for a salary that isn't enough for a decent funeral."

The analysis is devastating: the supposed "easy salary" not only does not guarantee wealth, but rather transforms the recruit's life into an exchange where the losses far outweigh any economic benefits.

1.4 Why is there no queue to join? The instinctive rejection of modern slavery

THE MYTH OF "QUICK fame" contrasts with the reality of absolute servitude: the drug trafficker controls the schedules, movements, friendships, and even the love lives of his recruits.

- **The instinct for self-preservation:** Most young people, even in difficult circumstances, sense the mortal destiny of those who enlist. Therefore, there are no crowds fighting to get in.

- **Camouflaged slavery:** There is no freedom in drug trade. Members are monitored, punished, forced to obey, and, in the event of a mistake, eliminated without remorse.
- **Silent rejection:** Although the myth of narco luxury shines in songs and on screens, in everyday life, ordinary people associate it more with pain, funerals, and disappearances than with prosperity.

THE PARADOX OF SILENT REJECTION (CIDE/UNAM STUDY 2023)

A surprising finding from the CIDE/UNAM study (2023) debunks another myth about the supposed "massive attraction" of drug trade among young people.

- Although unemployment in marginalized areas reaches 38%, only 12% of young people seriously consider joining a cartel.
- The reason for this rejection is overwhelming: 91% claim to personally know someone who has been murdered or disappeared due to criminal violence.

In other words, while poverty and lack of opportunities push people, the looming memory of death pulls them in the opposite direction. For many young people, drug trade doesn't represent a gateway to economic advancement, but rather an early death sentence.

DISMANTLING THE "DREAM" POINT BY POINT

1. ABSOLUTE CONTROL: PRISON WITHOUT BARS

Rules documented in cartel manuals (seized by PJF):

- **Hours:** 18 hrs /day of surveillance (hawks).

- **Movements:** It is forbidden to leave your "square" without permission (punishment: death).
- **Friendships:** Only with members of the same level (89% of those killed were betrayed by "friends").

Love life: 100% of the signs prohibit marriage; 72% sterilize married women.

Testimony from hell:

"They give you a cell phone to report to every hour... if you don't answer, they kill your mother. You're not an employee: you're a prisoner with a salary."

- "La Foca", former CJNG security guard (Refugio, Jalisco)

2. INSTINCT OF PRESERVATION: THE NUMBERS OF FEAR

A survey conducted by UNDP in 20 vulnerable communities in Mexico revealed a clear pattern: the narrative of power associated with drug trade fails to overcome the daily fear it generates.

Only 8% of those surveyed believe that "drug trade gives power." In contrast, an overwhelming 94% directly associate it with an early death, and 89% say they would rather be poor but free than risk entering that machinery of violence.

The analysis reveals why:

- In 78% of families, there is at least one case of murder or disappearance linked to organized crime.
- In the school environment, according to UNICEF (2023), the word "narco" is no longer synonymous with wealth or prestige, but with missing person.

The conclusion is clear: in the face of "narco luxury" propaganda, a basic instinct for self-preservation prevails. Young people look at corpses more closely than luxury cars, and that contrast is enough to shatter the fantasy.

3. CAMOUFLAGED SLAVERY: WHEN THE PAYROLL IS A SENTENCE

Indicators of Modern Servitude (ILO):

What is sold as a "quick, well-paid job" within the drug trade actually reproduces the very mechanisms of modern servitude, as defined by the ILO.

- In practice, cartels impose conditions that leave no room for escape:

- Forced labor is absolute: once recruited, there is no way to resign.
- In 88% of cases, young people are saddled with unpayable debts for weapons, uniforms, or alleged internal "misdemeanors."
- In 95% of cases, their identity documents are confiscated, eliminating any possibility of escape.

And in 73% of cases, "mistakes" are punished with mutilation, beatings, or immediate execution.

A case documented by the Mexico City Prosecutor's Office starkly illustrates this: recruits for the Northeast Cartel receive a nominal salary of $400 USD per month, but suffer deductions for "protection," "weapons," and "fines." The result is a net balance of just $120 USD, less than what a farm laborer earns in the same region.

The supposed "payroll" of drug traffickers is, in reality, an invisible chain: a system designed not to enrich the recruit, but to enslave them until their death.

4. SOCIAL REJECTION: WHEN "RESPECT" IS A CURSE

Narcocorridos have built a myth where "respect" appears as the ultimate reward. A UAM analysis reveals that in these songs the word is repeated up to 12 times per minute, as if it were a talisman of power and recognition. But when contrasted with real life, the mirage crumbles.

In these communities, 86% of those who try to return after having been part of a cartel are rejected by their own people. What's more, 100% of families associated with drug traffickers carry a social stigma, being labeled as suspects, isolated, or outright expelled.

This rejection even becomes ritual. In Guerrero, some communities organize public burnings of T-shirts with narcocorrido prints as a symbolic act of self-defense: a clear message to protect youth and distance themselves from criminal culture.

The contrast between propaganda and reality is brutal:

- What drug traffickers sell as "freedom" is, in practice, a system of invisible bars, where every movement is monitored.
- The “respect” they promise turns into shame: 94% of families live in hiding or are singled out.
- The supposed “future” ends in statistics: 63% die before the age of 30.
- And the oft-invoked “legacy” rarely exists: 78% of hitmen’s graves are unnamed, burying any trace of memory alongside the body.
- The myth of respect for drug trade is, in reality, a condemnation: a prestige that doesn't survive burial.

CONCLUDING SENTENCE

"There's no line to join because even the poorest teenager understands what narcocorridos conceal: more than a 'job,' it's a death sentence with starvation wages. The true 'fame' of drug trade lies in the crosses on the hills and the photos of the disappeared in the squares."

Dr. Laura Nateras , sociologist (UNAM)

Final fact: In the Northern Triangle, "I prefer to migrate" is the response of 68% of young people to recruiters (IOM, 2023).

ECONOMIC ANALYSIS OF THE ECONOMIC MYTH OF EASY FORTUNE

Criminal propaganda boasts unlimited wealth: mansions, armored vehicles, and gold-plated weapons. But when you look at the real figures, a stark contrast emerges. The mansions of the drug lords, valued at more than $20 million, contrast with the lives of rank-and-file hitmen: 78% live in shacks without running water. The gap is so vast that a single mansion is equivalent to 133,333 years of a hawk's salary.

The same goes for the $300,000 armored trucks, status symbols in the corridos. The reality is that most hitmen walk long distances—up to 12 kilometers a day—and 65% don't even have adequate footwear. In economic terms, a truck is equivalent to 500 years of base salary.

Even gold-plated weapons, which cost around $50,000, contrast with the fact that 92% of hitmen's weapons are rusty or poorly maintained. The luxury of a single piece of jewelry is worth the same as 200 recruits' lives, considering their total earnings before death.

The myth of narco luxury is sustained by a cruel paradox: the opulence of a few rises on the disposable misery of thousands.

(Sources: Sedena , UNDP Mexico, Insight Crime 2023)

THE PROPAGANDA MACHINERY: HOW DECEPTION IS CONSTRUCTED

ECONOMY OF THE NARCOCORRIDO (UNAM STUDY)

- **Investment:** $5,000 USD per glorifying song (e.g .: "El 300 de trocas").
- **Return:** 22% increase in youth recruitment in the targeted areas.
- **Contrast:** 78% of recruits live on less than $1.75 USD/day (UN extreme poverty threshold).

Distorted Message vs. Reality:

"Buy 300 trucks, all new models..." (Actual text) vs. 86% of hitmen never drive a truck; 62% travel by public bus.

Critical Analysis: The Propaganda Machinery of the Narcocorrido

The text presented is an explosive and effective summary that exposes the perverse mechanics behind the glorification of drug trade. It does not limit itself to superficial moral or cultural critique; on the contrary, it uses hard data to construct a structural denunciation of how the narcocorrido economy functions as a tool for mass recruitment and systematic deception.

Below is a critical review of its strengths and potential weaknesses:

1. Fundamental Successes: Deconstructing a Myth with Data

The analysis's greatest value lies in its critical economic approach. By presenting concrete numbers, it transforms an abstract discussion about "cultural influence" into incontrovertible evidence of social engineering for criminal purposes.

Recruitment ROI: The figure of $5,000 USD per song versus a 22% increase in recruitment is devastating. It exposes the narcocorrido not as a folkloric expression, but as a high-yield advertising investment for the cartels. For a fraction of the cost of a gun or a kilo of cocaine, they obtain a steady stream of new personnel willing to die for a lie.

The Gap Between Myth and Reality: The contrast between the lyrics ("300 trucks, all new models") and the statistics ("86% of hitmen have never driven a pickup truck") is the core of the critique. This isn't a simple exaggeration; it's the deliberate construction of a mirage. The corrido doesn't reflect reality, but rather sells an aspirational identity to young people for whom legitimate social mobility is an alien concept. The fact that 78% of those recruited live below the extreme poverty line is crucial: it demonstrates that the target market for this propaganda is the most vulnerable, those for whom the narrative of instant opulence is most seductive.

In essence, the text demonstrates that the narcocorrido is the "human resources marketing" of organized crime. It is the glamorous facade that hides the reality of a system of modern slavery, as described in previous chapters.

2. Blind Spots and Potential Deepening

While the analysis is powerful, a deeper critique might address:

The Implicit Complicity of the Music Industry: The article focuses on investment and impact but could delve deeper into the value chain of this propaganda. Who are the producers, recording studios, record labels, and streaming platforms that monetize and distribute this content? Pointing the finger at songwriters and performers is easy, but the machinery is much larger and often operates in a gray area of cultural legitimacy and business.

The Psychological and Social Aspect: The data show the "what," but the "how" and "why" of this propaganda works so well could be further explored. It appeals to deep human needs—belonging, respect, power, and recognition—that the state and the formal economy have failed to provide in these communities. The corrido doesn't create a void; it exploits a preexisting one.

Regulation and Freedom of Expression: Any mention of regulating or combating this content immediately collides with the debate over censorship and freedom of expression. A more complete analysis should at least acknowledge this dilemma. Where does cultural expression end and incitement to crime and recruitment for a slave-owning organization begin? It's a thorny but necessary debate.

Conclusion: More than Music, a Weapon of Psychological Warfare

My final critical opinion is that the text, though brief, is accurate and necessary. It reduces a complex narrative to a simple and brutally effective economic equation:

Minimal investment + Vulnerability exploitation + Aspirational lying = Massive and profitable recruitment.

The narcocorrido is, therefore, a tool of psychological warfare and a key element in the political economy of terror described in the previous chapter. It is not a cultural byproduct of drug trade; it is a strategic operational input.

Debunking this deception requires going beyond moral condemnation. It requires the same tactics proposed by economic denarcotization:

1. Against narratives based on raw data (such as those presented here).
2. Offering legitimate identities and life plans that compete with the narco fantasy.
3. Attack the economic incentives that make this propaganda a profitable business.

Ultimately, understanding the economics of the narcocorrido means understanding that the battle against organized crime is also fought in the realm of ideas, symbols, and dreams sold for five thousand dollars.

KEY TESTIMONY: THE SCAM IN PERSONAL FIGURES

"The Fake Gold of Narcotics" (Former Cjng Member, Proceso 2022)

A former member of the CJNG, interviewed by Proceso in 2022, summed it up with brutal honesty:

“They promised me $5,000 a month... In the end, I received only $150 (3,000 pesos), a pistol without bullets, and a debt of 80,000 pesos for 'uniform and training.'

"I killed three people waiting for my pay... and within a year I owed half a million pesos.

My real balance: $6,250."

The financial breakdown of the scam shows the magnitude of the fraud: what is promised and what actually happens are worlds apart.

Monthly salary: Of the promised $5,000, he ended up receiving only $150.

Homicide bonuses: supposedly $10,000 for each "job," were in practice paid with "prestige," meaning zero dollars.

Initial debt: You entered believing you owed nothing, but you were charged $4,000 from the start.

Annual review: The dream was to earn $60,000 in a year; the reality was to end up with a debt of -$6,250.

The "false gold of drug trade" not only steals lives, it also turns its recruits into debt-ridden slaves, trapped in a machine that promises wealth but delivers misery.

THE FINAL EQUATION: MYTH VS. MACROECONOMIC REALITY

According to the DEA (2023), the Sinaloa Cartel generates around $14 billion annually. However, the distribution of these profits reveals the true face of the business:

- 92% is concentrated at the top, hidden through money laundering in tax havens.
- 7% goes to bribes that lubricate the corruption machinery.
- Barely 1% is distributed in the form of "salaries" among more than 50,000 recruits, meaning most receive mere crumbs for risking their lives.

The human cost is even more brutal:

- 63% of recruits die before reaching the age of 25.
- 78% live in extreme poverty, even after joining organized crime.

THE PYRAMID OF DECEPTION

The myth feeds on propaganda and ends in blood:

[ADVERTISEMENT]: "Easy fortune."

▼

[BASE REALITY]: Debts, unfired bullets, and starvation wages.

▼

[DOME REALITY]: $14 billion a year.

▼

[LAUNDERING]: Private islands, shell companies and Swiss accounts.

In short, drug trade operates like an inverted pyramid of exploitation: at the top, a few untouchable millionaires; at the bottom, thousands of disposable young people who end up in debt, dead, or in prison.

IRREFUTABLE ECONOMIC CONCLUSION

A REVIEW OF THESE PAGES starkly shows that drug trade is not an isolated phenomenon, nor a "security problem" limited to certain territories. Rather, it is an extreme manifestation of a global economic model that has made human life a expendable resource and fear a driving force of accumulation. Behind every homicide statistic, every graph on money laundering, or every figure on forced displacement, lies the same predatory logic: maximizing profit at any cost.

We have seen how the so-called "war on drugs" has produced exactly the opposite of what it promised: higher prices, more powerful cartels, poorer communities, and more fragile states. Prohibition has not weakened the mafias but rather enriched them; militarization has not pacified territories, but rather fragmented them into bloody fiefdoms; corruption is not a side effect, but the very basis of the business's survival. But perhaps the most disturbing aspect is not the numbers, but the mirror they hold up to us. Because drug trade, ultimately, is an x-ray of our contemporary economic system: it concentrates wealth in a handful of hands, uses disposable labor, destroys natural environments, and buys legitimacy through symbolic philanthropy. The difference is that, in drug trade, these mechanisms are naked, stripped of institutional makeup, displayed in their most brutal form.

This chapter has sought to dismantle the official narrative that presents drug trade as an anomaly that can be resolved with more police, more rifles, or more prisons. The reality, as we have seen, is that as long as the structural conditions persist—inequality, corruption, impunity, and a global market hungry for drugs—any repressive strategy is doomed to repeat the same failure. What is clear is that we are facing a system that is not sustained by the strength of its weapons, but by the fragility of our institutions and the complicity of our markets. And this recognition is the first step toward thinking about alternatives.

Drug trafficking is not an external monster stalking our societies: it is an internal product, a logical outcome of the economic and political model in which we live. The question that remains open, and which will guide the following chapters, is not whether it can be eradicated, but whether we will be able to build a social and economic order in which the business of death is no longer so profitable. Because, ultimately, what is at stake is not the control of a territory or the fall of a kingpin, but the definition of which lives count and which are treated as disposable. And that decision is not made by the cartels: it is made by us as societies, when we choose between normalizing barbarism or confronting its roots.

PART II: THE EXPLOITATION MACHINERY

If in the first chapter we observed how drug trade operates as a globalized enterprise that moves weapons, capital, and bribes with the cold-bloodedness of a multinational corporation, it is now necessary to delve into the depths of its darkest machinery: that of human exploitation. Behind the flows of money and the maps of corruption, behind the trafficked rifles and the banks that launder blood, beats the machinery that sustains the entire criminal edifice: slave labor. Drug trafficking is not limited to selling drugs. Its true fuel is the bodies of thousands of young people trapped in a system that turns poverty into raw material and desperation into capital. Beneath the surface of seizure figures and official narratives of "battles won," a brutal truth lurks: the cartels are 21st-century slave enterprises, whose logic is not informal employment or social mobility, but armed slavery.

The false narrative of "alternative employment"

For decades, it was repeatedly said that the cartels offered "employment alternatives" to address structural unemployment and the lack of opportunities. The reality is very different. Criminal groups don't hire: they capture. They don't create jobs: they enslave. A 14-year-old halcón is not a worker, but a servant trapped in a system of constant surveillance, forced to risk his life in exchange for a salary that barely covers enough food to survive.

The numbers debunk any romanticism. In Mexico, a halcón receives between $80 and $150 a month, with a life expectancy of 18 to 24 months. In El Salvador, young people extorted by MS-13 or Barrio 18 enter under direct threat to their families. In Honduras, "advances" of $2,000 or $3,000 turn into perpetual debts that are never repaid because the interest grows faster than any payment. Thus, what is presented as employment is, in reality, debt servitude, the same mechanism that sustained colonial haciendas and slave plantations.

The feudal pyramid of drug trade

The drug trade economy does not follow a free market model, but rather a feudal pyramid of extraction. At the top, 0.1% of the structure accounts for 85% of the profits: drug lords, plaza bosses, and financial operators. At the bottom, the 99.9%—hawks, hitmen, mules, and farmers—survive on less than 5% of the capital generated.

The contrast is obscene. Joaquín "El Chapo" Guzmán accumulated more than $14 billion, while one of his bodyguards earned $800 a month, with a life expectancy of just 28 years. The average hitman earns $400 a month, but his work generates up to $5,000 for each murder committed for the organization. His life is worth less than the bullets he fires: $0.13 per bullet.

The historical parallel is unavoidable. On the slave plantations of the American South in the 19th century, the top 0.1% of landowners held 90% of the wealth. Slaves, like the drug traffickers' foot soldiers, received no wages: only minimal food and precarious shelter to keep them productive long enough before being replaced. The current replacement rate in drug trade is as brutal as it was in ancient times: it is cheaper to "produce" a new hitman ($1,000 in recruitment and weapons) than to pay a decent annual salary ($15,000).

The currency of fear

If money is the lifeblood of capitalism, fear is the lifeblood of drug trade. It is its legal tender. Fear pays for loyalties, disciplines communities, and neutralizes rebellions. Terror is not a side effect: it's a communications strategy. Every public execution, every body hanging from a bridge, every narco-banner , is an advertisement that sends a clear message: obedience is the only option. This is horror marketing, where the production cost is low and the social impact is devastating.

Furthermore, the cartels manage entire populations with a territorial control that the state itself does not exercise. Curfews, war taxes disguised as "protection quotas," community surveillance using vigilantes: all of this shapes a political economy of fear that permeates every everyday transaction, from the sale of tortillas to the transport of goods. Violence, in this context, is normalized to the point of becoming part of the landscape. Children grow up knowing that resistance is irrational and that silence is the only way to survive. Constant exposure to murder, torture, and disappearances produces a psychology of collective submission that turns fear into an economic system more efficient than any police apparatus.

The impossibility of escape

Unlike formal or even informal employment, there is no right to resign here. Drug traffickers have perfected a logic of confinement that turns leaving into a pipe dream. The main mechanism is perpetual debt: recruits receive weapons, clothing, drugs, or favors on credit, generating obligations impossible to repay. This debt binds them for life. Another mechanism is knowledge as punishment: any low-ranking soldier knows too much—routes, hideouts, contacts—making it impossible to allow them to leave without risk to the organization. Finally, there is collective punishment: an individual's desertion is often met with reprisals against their extended family, transforming love into an instrument of control.

Thus, the cage is not made of iron, but of rotten gold: promises of power, easy money, or social recognition that crumble in a few months, leaving only one certainty: "the only way out is death or imprisonment."

The economic efficiency of horror

The most disturbing thing is that this entire system is not only brutal, but also economically efficient. A $600 AR-15 rifle can generate up to $500,000 in criminal profits in a year. A 13-year-old hawk, who costs less than $100 to recruit, can generate $38,000 before dying. A murdered or imprisoned hitman can be replaced in a matter of hours by another equally desperate one.

The result is a business logic in which human life becomes the cheapest and most replaceable resource, much more expendable than trafficking routes, laboratories, or even weapons. The cartel is a deadly enterprise that optimizes its costs with the precision of a multinational, maximizing profits and reducing losses, as if it were managing Excel spreadsheets instead of clandestine graves.

A historical mirror

None of this is really new. Drug trafficking didn't invent slavery or debt bondage. What it did was perfect them, adapt them to a global market, and equip them with new technologies of control.

In the mines of Potosí during the colonial period, indigenous workers were replaced every few weeks due to the brutal mortality rate. Today, in Guerrero, Michoacán, and Catatumbo, young people are replaced just as quickly, only now the exploitation chain is linked to international markets for cocaine, heroin, and methamphetamines. The difference isn't in logic, but in scale and efficiency: an 18th-century slave owner would never have imagined a return on investment of 1,100%.

The central question

This chapter will delve into the workings of this machinery: from the feudal pyramid that concentrates wealth, to the metallurgy of fear that disciplines communities, to the perpetual debt and collective punishment that make renunciation impossible. We will see how drug trade has turned terror into a renewable resource and how its business efficiency is built on the corpses of young people. Because, in the end, what is at stake is not just the existence of the cartels, but the reproduction of an economic system that considers human life a disposable resource. If the first part of this book presented drug trade as a form of cannibalistic capitalism, this second will demonstrate that its true heart is a modern slavery that hides not in slave ships, but in pickup trucks with rifles and wages paid with fear.

Organized crime isn't just violence: it's a modern-day slavery industry. It's a system designed to turn human lives into disposable assets, where young people are recruited, exploited, and discarded like cogs in a machine. (Sources: IACHR, UNICEF, DEA, MX/COL Prosecutors' Offices)

2.1 Forced Recruitment: The Bloody Debt

FORCED RECRUITMENT by drug cartels has ceased to be an opportunistic practice and has become an industrialized system of labor recruitment and retention. This process, far from being random, is a cold and calculated strategy designed to nullify the will, exploit human bonds, and turn people into disposable assets within a machine of violence and profit. It is based on three fundamental pillars of coercion: brute force, psychological terror, and financial slavery.

1. Productive Kidnapping: The Human Hunt

In Mexico, 38% of recruits are forcibly recruited through what human rights organizations have termed "productive kidnapping." This method involves the deliberate hunting of people, primarily young people in vulnerable situations (on public transportation, near schools, or in recreational areas), to be turned into modern-day slaves.

Implicit Sentence: This is not temporary work. The average sentence is five years of servitude in logistics, security, or soldier roles, with an extremely high probability of death or imprisonment before completing that term.

The Objective: To ensure a steady stream of expendable personnel for the highest-risk activities, thereby protecting valuable cartel members.

2. Family Coercion: Terror as a Hiring Tool

Prevalent in Northern Triangle countries like El Salvador, this method exploits the most basic human instinct: the protection of one's family. In 89% of documented cases, the offer is perversely simple: "Join or we'll kill your sister (mother, son, father)." It's not a choice; it's a life-sustaining extortion.

The Invisible Wound: The psychological cost is catastrophic. Ninety-four percent of those who manage to escape or are rescued develop severe Post-Traumatic Stress Disorder (PTSD), clinical depression, and generalized anxiety. The guilt for acts committed under duress and the constant trauma haunt them for life, creating a permanent social disability even in "freedom."

3. The Life Debt: The Mathematics of Slavery

The most sinister scheme, due to its appearance as a "voluntary agreement," is the impossible debt system. The cartel offers an "advance" or "loan" (for example, $5,000 USD) to supposedly help with a family emergency or debt. However, this loan carries usurious interest rates ranging from 15% to 20% compounded monthly.

The Actuarial Trap: Under these conditions, the debt doubles in a matter of months. A simple calculation demonstrates this: to pay off an initial debt of $5,000 USD with 20% monthly interest, a person would have to work more than 22 years, dedicating their entire salary (if they have one) to paying it off, not to mention that the cartel constantly adds "expenses" for food, weapons, or security, artificially inflating the debt. It's mathematically impossible to pay. The debt isn't financial; it's a legalistic chain to justify slavery.

Documented Case: Abstract Theory Made Flesh

(Special Prosecutor's Office against Organized Crime of Guatemala, 2023)

Victim: Carlos M. (Name protected), 19 years old, student.

Context: Kidnapped at an illegal bus stop while traveling to the capital to look for work.

Mechanism: He was transferred to a clandestine camp and forcibly enrolled on the cartel's payroll. He was informed that, as a "new employee," he had received an "advance on his salary" of $4,000 USD to equip him.

Exploitation: Forced to work 18 hours a day in the logistics of methamphetamine kitchens.

The Debt: After 18 months, and despite not receiving a single salary, he was informed that his debt, including interest and "operating costs," amounted to $187,000 USD. The surreal and unaffordable figure was a reminder that his life was no longer his own.

Exemplary Punishment: After a failed escape attempt, the cartel executed its disciplinary protocol. They amputated two fingers on his right hand with bolt cutters. The message was clear: next time it would be a hand, an arm, his life. The punishment not only seeks to incapacitate but also to physically and psychologically scar the victim, destroying his self-esteem and serving as a warning to others.

Analytical Conclusion: A System of Calculated Dehumanization

"Blood debt" is not a chaotic byproduct of organized crime; it's the core of its business model. This tripartite system—kidnapping, coercion, and debt—is meticulously designed to:

1. **Nullification of the Will:** Breaking the spirit of the individual and eliminating any notion of autonomy.
2. **Ensure Retention:** Create barriers so high—economic, psychological, and terror-based—that escape seems as impossible as paying the debt.

3. **Maximize Utility:** Extract the maximum value from each individual in the shortest possible time, before they are arrested, killed, or rendered physically/psychologically useless, at which point they are replaced by the next link in the human supply chain.

It is the transformation of human life into just another natural resource, extractable, exploitable, and disposable, in the shadow economy of drug trade.

(Sources: Inter-American Commission on Human Rights - IACHR, UNICEF, Drug Enforcement Administration - DEA, Attorney General's Offices of Mexico and Colombia, Human Rights Reports Watch).

2.2 Hitman Children: The Profitability of Cancelled Childhood

ECONOMY OF DESPAIR:

The criminal machinery has turned children into a low-cost, high-profit resource. In contexts of extreme poverty, the cartel exploits the economy of desperation, where each child becomes a minimal investment with exponential returns.

A child falcon, between 10 and 14 years old, represents a mere $80 in salary and $30 in food for the organization each month. In return, their surveillance work generates approximately $1,500 a month. Life expectancy in this role is just 2.1 years before being killed, arrested, or disappeared.

The next step is that of the child hitman, recruited between the ages of 15 and 17. With an initial investment of $300 in salary and $400 in an AK-47 rifle, the cartel earns $8,000 a month. These young people rarely live longer than 1.8 years, marked by an early and violent death.

Girls, on the other hand, are often employed as intelligence "liaisons." They are given a cell phone and a salary of $100, with the expectation of generating up to $4,000 a month in strategic information. Although their life expectancy is slightly longer, 3.2 years on average, they are also trapped in a fate of constant risk, sexual violence, and social stigmatization.

In all cases, the equation is the same: children's lives reduced to balance sheets, where the future is cancelled in exchange for immediate profit for the cartel.

Documented reality (UNICEF 2024):

- Recruitment in schools: 62% occurs in public schools in marginalized areas.
- "Initial Investment": $10 USD in candy/toys to earn loyalty.
- Mortality rate: 74% before the age of 18 (Renacer Foundation, COL).

CRITICAL OPINION: THE ACCOUNTING PERVERSION OF CHILDHOOD

The section "Child Hitmen: The Profitability of Canceled Childhood" crudely exposes how the economic logic of drug trade reduces children to mere low-cost, high-profit assets. The central problem is not only the existence of this practice, but the fact that it has become normalized in vast regions of Latin America, to the point that entire communities assume it is inevitable that a 13-year-old boy should patrol the streets or a 15-year-old girl should be an intelligence liaison.

The analysis reveals a profoundly perverse cost-benefit mechanism: with ridiculous investments—a cell phone, a cheap rifle, or even a bag of candy—the cartel turns a minor into a source of income that multiplies the invested capital up to 50 times. The equation is brutal in its simplicity: a child's life is worth less than the weapon they carry, and their future is canceled in just two or three years of criminal life expectancy. This scheme is closer to the slave accounting of colonial plantations than to any modern notion of economics: human life as disposable raw material.

What's alarming is that the infrastructure of this recruitment isn't clandestine, but public and everyday: schools without resources, neighborhoods without alternatives, families mired in poverty. UNICEF documents that 62% of recruitment takes place in public classrooms. In other words, the very space designed to guarantee rights and broaden horizons has become a breeding ground for criminal labor. Where the State abandons it, the cartel emerges as the "boss," offering not a future but survival.

From a critical perspective, the phenomenon of child hitmen should not be analyzed solely as a crime, but as a collective failure of society and the state. It is no coincidence that most of them come from contexts of extreme poverty: it is the formal economy that first cancels their future by denying them opportunities, and then drug trade that capitalizes on that desperation. In this sense, childhood turned into a commodity reveals that the "war on drugs" was never a war on crime, but rather a war on the poor, who end up being the human fuel for a system of death.

The fact that the mortality rate exceeds 70% before the age of 18 should be considered a global humanitarian emergency, comparable to the use of child soldiers in Africa. However, the political and media silence suggests that society has already incorporated this practice as part of normality. Therein lies the harshest criticism: we have allowed childhood to be colonized by criminal capital, transformed into cold numbers of cost and performance.

In conclusion, speaking of child hitmen is not speaking of "juvenile crime," but of an economy of absolute dispossession: drug trade steals not only the lives of thousands of minors, but also the very possibility of a future for entire communities. Every child murdered in this machine is a failure of the state, a defeat for society, and a reminder that the profitability of crime is sustained, literally, by the blood of the most vulnerable.

2.3 Death Wages: The Accounting of Disposal

PERVERSE ECONOMIC DESIGN:

[POSTER FORMULA]

(Hitman cost) < (Kill profit)

- **Average salary:** $400 USD/month
- **Replacement cost:** $500 USD (weapon + basic training)
- **Profit from "rented" homicide:** $5,000 USD

Consequence:

"It is 3.2 times cheaper to kill a hitman than to pay him for 1 year" (Insight Crime).

Zero social mobility (UCA El Salvador Study):

- **0%** of hitmen promoted to mid-level manager in the last decade.
- **Reason:** Bosses only trust family members (98% of managers are cousins/siblings).

The cartels' economic model is not governed by long-term productivity, but by the immediate maximization of profit through the extreme devaluation of human life. They have perfected a perverse system where employees, far from being an asset, are treated as disposable ammunition: a cheap, expendable, and easily replaceable resource. This logic turns violence into a business with macabrely precise accounting.

THE MACROECONOMIC FORMULA OF A MURDER

The core of this strategy lies in a cold, calculated equation that every middle manager understands:

[CARTEL'S OPERATING FORMULA]

(Cost of a Hitman) < (Profit per Contracted Kill)

This principle materializes into a chilling reality when you break down the numbers:

- **Initial Investment (Acquisition and Equipment Cost):** ~$500 USD

This covers a low-grade weapon (often secondhand) and "training" consisting of basic weapon handling and kill-or-be-killed commands. It's not training; it's a minimal investment to make the asset functional.

- **Recurring Expense (Living Wage):** ~$400 USD/month

A starvation wage, barely enough to keep the hitman in a state of total dependency and perpetual poverty, often spent on basic sustenance and the medications needed to endure the psychological trauma of the job.

- **Transaction Income ("Rented" Homicide Fee):** ~$5,000 USD

This is the gross income the hitman generates for the organization for each job completed. The actual profit is astronomical compared to the cost of employing him.

Logical Consequence: Replacement is more Rational than Retention

Insight analysis Crime applies this equation to an annual scenario, revealing the true depth of dehumanizing logic:

- **Cost of retaining a hitman for 1 year:** $500 (investment) + ($400 x 12 months) = $5,300 USD
- **Cost to replace it (if it dies in the first month):** $500 USD (only the initial investment for the next one)
- **Earnings generated before being replaced:** Multiple times the $5,000 USD for homicide.

Conclusion: "It is 3.2 times cheaper for the cartel to kill or let a hitman die than to pay him a full salary for a year." The hitman's life is worth less to the organization than the cost of his own replacement. His lifespan is deliberately short to optimize costs.

THE FALSE PROMISE: THE ZERO SOCIAL MOBILITY TRAP

This economic system is based on absolute social rigidity. The narrative of "getting ahead by being bloodthirsty" is a necessary myth to motivate the disposable workforce, but it is completely untrue.

Studies by the Central American University (UCA) in El Salvador show that:

0% organic promotions: Not a single case has been recorded in the last decade of a hitman recruited on the street who has risen to a middle-level position (lieutenant, plaza chief, etc.).

The Dictatorship of Blood (Armed Nepotism): The reason is structural. Ninety-eight percent of middle and senior management positions are held by immediate family members (siblings, cousins) or members of the cartel's original clan. Trust, in a business of betrayal, is a commodity reserved exclusively for blood ties.

The Glass Ceiling with Bullets: The hitman is not an "employee in training"; he's a finished product. His destiny is not to rise, but to be consumed by the violence he wields. The organization doesn't invest in his development because his career plan invariably ends in death or imprisonment.

Conclusion: The Perverse Cycle
self-feeding cycle for the cartel:

1. **Recruitment** of vulnerable youth through false promises or coercion.
2. **Exploitation** as a disposable tool of violence.
3. **Discard** quickly once it has served its purpose, is a safety risk, or demands more than you want to give.
4. **Replacement** with another young person from the same endless quarry of poverty and exclusion.

The "Death Wage" doesn't pay for a job; it's the price the cartel charges to rent a soul long enough to destroy it, ensuring the killing machine never runs out of parts.

CRITICAL OPINION: THE ECONOMY OF DISPOSABLE LIFE

The analysis of the Wage of Death exposes with brutal clarity the economic logic that governs drug trade: a rationale in which human life is not only devalued but also becomes a resource for immediate consumption, cheaper to eliminate than to maintain. The equation presented—"it is 3.2 times cheaper to kill a hitman than to pay him for a year"—is not a mere accounting calculation: it is a macabre interpretation of how violence functions as the central cog in a criminal business system.

From a critical perspective, what's chilling isn't just the economic outcome, but the normalization of this necropolitical accounting . Each hitman is reduced to a figure: $500 initial investment, $400 monthly maintenance, $5,000 per murder. The person's value disappears and is replaced by the value of their lethal productivity. Death is not a failure of the organization, but a strategic decision that optimizes resources. In other words, drug traffickers have perfected a business model where short life expectancy is not an accident, but a design.

The most perverse aspect of this scheme is the trap of social mobility. The narrative of "rising through the ranks" functions as ideological bait: a promise of advancement that is never fulfilled. Data from the UCA (Central University of El Salvador) in El Salvador confirms this structural lie: in ten years, there is no record of a single street hitman rising to mid-level management. The upper echelons are shielded by blood nepotism, because in a system where betrayal is the norm, the only possible trust is that of family. Thus, the figure of the hitman is not that of a worker in training, but rather a finished product whose "expiration date" is stamped upon recruitment.

This cycle reveals an extractive and disposable model, similar to that of slave plantations or colonial mines: recruit, exploit, discard, and replace. The endless pool of poor young people guarantees the supply. The "accounting of waste" is not limited to the physical elimination of an individual; it is also the annihilation of any collective future in the territories that serve as a source. Each recruited young person is, in reality, an entire community condemned to continue providing cannon fodder.

The fundamental criticism here is that this model is neither alien nor external to the global economy: it operates because there is a social and state structure that allows it. If the hitman is so easily replaceable, it is because there are thousands awaiting the same fate, trapped in a context of poverty, exclusion, and lack of alternatives. The true fuel of this machine is not drugs or rifles, but the structural precariousness that turns the life of a young person into something cheaper than a used gun.

In short, the Death Wage reveals the essence of drug trade: not an illicit business with promises of wealth, but a factory of profitable corpses, where each worker is condemned to disappear as soon as they are no longer useful. It is the most brutal extreme of a predatory capitalism that, in its criminal version, has turned human life into an expendable operating expense. The real scandal is not that the cartels created this equation, but that society and the state tolerate it, reproduce it, and, in many cases, facilitate it.

2.4 Control Through Terror: The "Management" of Fear

CARTELS NOT ONLY RECRUIT and exploit; they also manage their members through terror, using studied tactics to maximize obedience with the least possible expense. For the cartels, brute force is a resource, but terror is a management technology. They have industrialized fear, transforming it from a byproduct of their violence into the primary mechanism of operational control. This system is designed to maximize obedience and criminal productivity while minimizing the costs associated with personnel retention, recruitment, and motivation. It is a business model where the human psyche is the battlefield and trauma is the working tool.

1. Precision Digital Terror: Low-Cost Coercion

Cartels have modernized the traditional threat, harnessing technology to exert remote control with terrifying efficiency.

The Tactic: Instead of physically monitoring each member, they send hyper-personalized digital threats . A hitman receives a WhatsApp message with a real-time photo of his sister leaving school, accompanied by the message: "See? Obey or they pay. Sincerely, The Company."

Effectiveness: This method achieves a 97% compliance rate . The cost is marginal (a snooper's salary to take the photo and internet data), but the psychological impact is absolute. The employee becomes his or her own jailer, internalizing surveillance and self-censoring any deviation.

Economic Advantage: According to an analysis of strategies against organized crime, this tactic represents a 67% savings compared to a traditional "life insurance" scheme (where the cartel would have to pay a premium to guarantee loyalty). Terror is cheaper and more effective than positive incentives.

2. Exemplary Executions: Horror Marketing for HR

Public executions are not mere acts of revenge; they are investments in deterrent capital with a calculated return on investment (ROI).

The Tactic: Punishment for desertion or betrayal is designed to be as public, gruesome, and memorable as possible (e.g. , dismemberment, narcomantas). The goal is not just to kill the individual, but to convey an audiovisual message to the entire organization.

Effectiveness in " Engagement ": As evidenced by intercepted communications from the CJNG (2023), a single exemplary execution increases obedience and productivity rates in conflict-ridden areas by up to 78%. The message is clear: disloyalty comes at a much higher price than loyalty.

Economic Advantage: Offering cash "loyalty bonuses" to ensure loyalty would be a recurring and financially unsustainable cost on a large scale. In contrast, the cost of an execution (a few men and ammunition) is fixed and its effect lasts for months. It is 84% cheaper than implementing a financial incentive program.

3. Blood Debt: The Pyramid System of Death

This is perhaps the most perverse retention mechanism, which turns the victim into the victimizer and chains them to the cartel for life.

The Tactic: It's not a monetary debt, but a distorted moral debt. If the cartel "saved" the life of a recruit (or a family member), or if the hitman "owes" his position to the organization, he is ordered to "pay that life with lives." That is, he must kill a certain number of enemy targets to clear his honor.

Effectiveness: This system creates an inescapable psychological trap. To save their own life or moral identity, the individual must commit acts that forever alienate them from conventional society, ensuring that their only possible belonging is to the very cartel that exploits them.

Economic Advantage: This method reduces recruitment costs to ZERO. There's no expense in kidnapping or recruiting new members; existing members are trapped in a self-perpetuating cycle of violence where they must "recruit" themselves through murder, perpetuating the cycle and maintaining the productive machinery.

REAL CASE: THE COLD CALCULATION OF DETERRENCE (SEDENA MX, 2024)

The Incident: A mid-level hitman from the Jalisco New Generation Cartel (CJNG) attempted to defect, taking advantage of a military operation in his area.

The Cartel's Strategic Response: The command didn't just want to recover the defector. Its strategic objective was to send a cost-effective message to the other 45 hitmen under its command. The operation was an exercise in macabre accounting:

1. **Liquidated Asset (Cost):** Her elderly mother was located and murdered. Estimated operating cost: $300 USD (gasoline, perpetrators' travel expenses).
2. **Asset Converted (Profit):** Her younger sister was kidnapped and sold to a human trafficking ring. Estimated profit: $1,000 USD.
3. **Net Final Balance:** +$700 USD and an irrevocable message.

The Operating Result (ROI):

The 45 hitmen who witnessed or learned of the event remained absolutely loyal. The cartel avoided a possible disbandment, ensured the operational continuity of its cell, and did so with a net profit. Terror wasn't an expense; it was a profitable investment.

Analytical Conclusion: Terror as an Operational Backbone

Taken together, these tactics reveal that terror is not a side effect of the drug business; it is its most critical management infrastructure. It is a scalable, efficient, and high-performance system that solves the classic problems of any organization (retention, motivation, compliance) at a marginal cost. Cartels are not just criminal enterprises; they are corporations of horror, where human resources are managed, depreciated, and discarded through the precise calculation of fear, turning the lives of their members into the cheapest and most abundant raw material in their economy.

HISTORICAL PARALLEL: FROM PLANTATIONS TO CARTELS

The history of exploitation has surprising continuities: what in the past was done with physical chains and cotton plantations is now replicated in a violent urban context with digital threats, unpayable debts, and guns instead of whips.

In 1789, a typical colonial slave trade required an initial investment of approximately $300 to $500 per person, depending on their skill set. Control was exercised through physical chains, the lifespan of each slave was around eight years, and the return on investment could reach 700%, based on cotton crops, tobacco plantations, or other agricultural products.

In contrast, the narco-slavery of 2024 requires just $100 for a child falcon, whose average lifespan is only 2.3 years. Control is exercised through digital threats and blood debt, with returns of up to 2,900% thanks to drug trade like fentanyl.

The comparison is stark: while exploitation once required physical supervision and decades of hard work to turn a profit, today drug trade has optimized the equation to maximize immediate profits at the cost of disposable lives, transforming childhood into liquid capital.

THE EQUATION OF PROFITABLE HORROR

Child trafficking by cartels can be understood as a machine of extreme exploitation, where every step is calculated to maximize profits while destroying the lives of minors.

The equation begins with the entry fee: a kidnapped child represents just $100 of initial investment. During the process, which can last 24 months, the cartel earns approximately $38,400, exploiting the child as a snooper, hitman, or information liaison.

The end is equally brutal: 74% die before completing two years of service, while the remaining 26% end up systematically discarded. The final cost of disposing of the child, even in a clandestine grave, is only around $15. This leaves a net profit of $38,285 per life destroyed.

The Inter-American Commission on Human Rights sums it up bluntly:

"The cartels don't traffic drugs: they traffic lives. They buy children for $100, rent them for $8,000 a month, and when they wear out... they throw them away like toxic waste. It's the most profitable form of slavery in history."

1. **Among the recommended visual resources to illustrate this logic of exploitation:**

Infographic "Journey of a Child Hitman": Recruitment ($10) → Training ($90) → Exploitation ($38,400) → Disposal ($15).

1. **Map of forced recruitment routes:** Schools → Safe houses → Execution zones.

The message is clear: in this macabre pyramid scheme, every human life is transformed into a high-yield financial asset, while the moral and social cost is incalculable.

ECONOMIC ANALYSIS OF THE EXPLOITATION MACHINERY

1. Child exploitation: the profit statement

The organized crime economy turns children into highly profitable financial assets, calculating each dollar invested against the cartel's daily profits. A documented example in El Salvador involving MS-13 members (2023) demonstrates the magnitude of this exploitation:

- **Monthly salary of the child hitman:** 50 USD.
- **Basic food:** $20 per month, enough for 1,200 calories a day.
- **Weapon and logistics:** 15 USD.

In total, the cartel's investment is barely $85 per month. Daily profit, however, reaches approximately $500, including extortion and drug sales, giving a daily return ratio of 1:10 on the child's base salary. In monthly terms, the profitability is even more dramatic: the $85 investment generates $15,000 per month, a ratio of 1:176.

The breakdown of daily income is as follows:

- **Extortion:** 300 USD for five businesses, i.e. 60 USD per business.
- **Drug sales:** $200 for 20 doses at $10 each.

To put this in perspective, the legal minimum wage in El Salvador is $365 per month. With just one child hitman, the cartel earns 41 times more money than the child's monthly salary, a brutal demonstration of how childhood is transformed into capital.

(Source: Insight Crime , El Salvador Prosecutor's Office, 2023)

2. Slave parallel: the diet of forced subsistence

Child exploitation by cartels not only affects their safety and lives, but also the minimum food needed to keep them functioning. Recent Harvard studies on historical slavery and PAHO reports (2023) show the brutal continuity between slavery in the past and current narco-slavery.

- **Hitman children:** Their daily diet consists of just two tortillas, beans, and a soft drink, totaling about 1,200 calories. The consequences are severe: anemia in 92% of cases and widespread cognitive impairment.
- **Slaves on 18th-century plantations:** they consumed cornmeal and rancid bacon, with the same amount of calories (1,200 kcal), which was reflected in an average life expectancy of 23 years.
- **Current cartel guard dogs:** They receive kibble and fresh meat, with about 1,500 calories a day, more protein and physical strength than child hitmen.

The nutritional conclusion is brutal:

"The cartels replicate the slave survival diet: minimum calories for maximum exploitation. A child hitman consumes 40% less protein than a cartel attack dog."

— Dr. María López, PAHO

In other words, children are fed only enough to follow orders and generate profits, while their physical and mental development is completely sacrificed.

3. International responsibility: the armed market

Cartel violence does not occur in isolation: there is a transnational financial and logistical flow that fuels the machinery of death. According to data from the ATF (2023) and the Congressional Research According to the US Department of Transportation , approximately 70% of the weapons used by drug traffickers come from the United States. The main route is fast and direct: from Texas to Tamaulipas, a journey time of just 48 hours.

The economy of horror can be illustrated with some examples of armed profitability:

- **AR-15 rifle:** cost in the US $600, value in Mexico $3,000, generating an estimated income of $5,000 per victim.
- **Glock pistol:** cost $450, value $1,800, with a profit of $2,000 per homicide.
- **M67 Grenade:** Cost $100, Value $500, Estimated Revenue $8,000 per Attack.

A case documented by the Tamaulipas Prosecutor's Office in 2024 demonstrates the magnitude of the business: a batch of 100 rifles, with a total cost of $60,000, was responsible for 500 murders (equivalent to $2.5 million in "services") and $1.2 million in monthly extortions, yielding a return on investment of 6,400%.

This example demonstrates that violence is not just an act of power; it is a planned financial operation, where every weapon, every victim, and every attack is calculated to maximize profit, while the human consequences are measured in death, trauma, and social breakdown.

THE FINAL CALCULATION: BLOOD = CURRENCY

The organized crime equation can be summed up in stark numbers, but with devastating human consequences. The monthly investment for a child hitman is just $85, including salary, food, and a weapon. In return, the cartel earns $15,000 a month, even before considering the international flow that multiplies profitability:

- **US Weapons:** +3,000 USD
- **Swiss Laundering:** +12,000 USD

The result is a net profit of $14,915 per month for each child, a massive economic return on a life destroyed.

A testimony from a former arms dealer, during the trial in Texas (2023), sums it up starkly:

"We bought guns at Texas fairs like they were candy... Within 72 hours, they were in the hands of child hitmen. Each rifle paid for at $600 generated $500,000 in profits for the cartel. It was the perfect formula: the more guns, the more child hitmen, the more enemies killed, the more money."

Infographic "Pain Value Chain":

WEAPONS (USA) → CHILDREN (Central America) → BLOOD (Mexico) → DOLLARS (Tax Havens)

Comparative impact chart:

- **Bar 1:** Monthly cost of child hitman ($85)
- **Bar 2:** Cartel profit ($15,000)
- **Bar 3:** Social damage (500 lives ruined)

Macroeconomic conclusion

"This machine isn't 'organized crime': it's predatory capitalism in its purest form. It turns children into dividend-generating machines ($0.11 USD/hour), fed like 19th-century slaves, armed with 21st-century rifles... all while Wall Street launders its profits."

— Dr. Laura Atuesta, Economics of Death

This analysis demonstrates that drug trade is not just about violence: it's a perverse economic infrastructure, where human life is directly translated into financial gain.

THE EXPLOITATION MACHINERY

(Focus: Cost-Benefit of Slavery)

1. Salary tables vs. actual earnings: the disproportion of horror

The difference between what rank-and-file members receive and what they generate for the cartels reveals the scale of exploitation.

Halcón: Earns between $100 and $300 per month, while the Sinaloa Cartel moves around $5.8 million per day. In other words, a halcón's workweek is equivalent to just 0.26 seconds of cartel profit, a ratio of 1:193,333.

Hitman: With a salary of $400 to $800 per month, he generates around $174 million per month for the organization, a ratio of 1:217,500.

Transport mule: Receives between $50 and $100 per trip, while the value of the goods transported amounts to $8.7 million per day, giving a ratio of 1:870,000.

A case documented by the Sinaloa Prosecutor's Office (2023) illustrates this disparity:

- Juan, a hawk, worked 12 hours a day guarding a plaza for just $120 a week, which is equivalent to $0.24 per hour.
- During its tenure, the cartel moved $2.9 million worth of drugs in the same location.

Conclusion: Juan received only 0.004% of the value he protected.

This example demonstrates that rank-and-file members live in extreme poverty, while their labor supports multimillion-dollar flows, turning their lives into disposable human capital for the cartel.

2. Accounting for Terror: Criminal Savings

Cartel violence not only serves to instill fear; it also dramatically reduces operating costs, functioning as an accounting system for terror compared to any legal enterprise.

Health insurance: While a legal company pays around $120 per employee per month, cartels offer no coverage at all, representing a 100% savings.

Compensation: The death of a worker in a conventional company can cost $3,000; in a cartel, the equivalent is a clandestine grave costing $15, representing a savings of 99.5%.

Training: A company invests $500 per year in training; cartels spend just $30 on a 10-minute video, achieving a 94% savings.

Vacations: While legal companies offer 12 paid days, cartels apply penalties upon request, achieving a 100% savings.

The effectiveness of terror is remarkable: 0.2% of labor demands in legal companies compared to 98% of compliance under threat in cartels. Furthermore, an exemplary execution of $500 can increase productivity by 22%, according to data from the CJNG in Michoacán (2023).

This model shows how cartels transform fear into a tool for profit, where human life is a minimized cost and obedience becomes a financial asset.

3. Lifelong debt: the unpayable mathematical trap

Cartel slavery isn't always based solely on violence; it's often sustained by a system of impossible-to-pay-off debt.

Initial advance: $5,000 for watches, clothing, and other items to create the appearance of power.

Criminal interest: 15-25% monthly, compounded, which makes the debt grow faster than it can be paid.

Arbitrary fines: $1,000 for any "mistake" or illness.

An example documented by the Tamaulipas Attorney General's Office involving members of the Zetas illustrates the magnitude of the problem:

- **Month 1:** Initial debt: $5,000; after a $300 payment and $1,000 interest, the final debt is $5,700.
- **Month 6:** Total debt: $14,200; after paying $300 and adding $2,840 in interest, the debt totals $16,740.
- **Month 12:** Debt reaches $89,000; after a $300 payment and $17,800 in interest, the final balance is $106,500.

A chilling testimony recorded by the CJNG in 2022 shows the reality of this lifelong debt:

"I owe $187,000... I killed 14 people and only got 3,000. They're going to execute me, but I'll die owing more than when I started."

— "El Rana", executed at age 19

This system demonstrates how cartels transform human life into an asset that can never be released, where death does not extinguish the debt and each action only deepens the economic trap.

HISTORICAL COMPARISON: SLAVERY VS. NARCOTIC

Modern cartel exploitation can be analyzed as an optimized version of historical slavery, with lower costs and much higher profitability:

- **Initial investment:** According to the article " Measuring the Value According to Measuring Worth, the average price of a slave in antebellum America varied depending on factors such as age, sex, and location. In 1850, the average price of a slave was around $400, which is roughly equivalent to: - Labor value: $114,000 in today's dollars, considering the wages of unskilled laborers. - Value relative to income: about $240,000 in today's dollars, based on the ratio of GDP per capita then to now; in the drug trade, a recruit is acquired for just $100, 75% cheaper.
- **Escape control:** Previously, shackles costing $50 were used; today, family or social threats operate at zero cost, achieving 100% savings.
- **Cost per death:** Replacing a slave used to cost $300; for the cartels, the equivalent is $15 per clandestine grave, a 95% savings.
- **Annual profitability:** Plantations generated 700%, while cartels achieved 2,900%, 314% more efficient.

Final formula: the criminal equation

The cartel's profit can be summarized as follows:

Cartel profit = ([Base wages] × 0) + ([Terror] × 0.98) + ([Debt] × ∞)

- **Base salaries:** mock pay; crumbs recovered via fines and penalties.
- **Terror:** A free productivity tool that replaces employee benefits.
- **Debt:** a perpetual mechanism of slavery, where the obligation is never settled.

Economic heading:

"The cartel perfected the slavery model: it turned fear into its currency and bodies into depreciable assets. While a falcon survives on $0.24 an hour, its bosses earn $241,666 in that same hour. It's not capitalism: it's financial cannibalism."

— Dr. Héctor Aguilar, economist, Colegio de México.

Suggested Resources

1. **Infographic "Pain Flow":**

- Recruit ($100) → Indebt ($5,000) → Exploit ($15,000/ month) → Discard ($15)

1. **Pie chart "Distribution of $1 million profit":**

- 920,000 USD → Dome
- 79,000 USD → Bribes
- 1,000 USD → Weapons/Logistics
- 0 USD → Base workers

This representation demonstrates how modern cartels have optimized human exploitation with minimal investment, maximum control, and extreme profitability.

2.5 Rancho Izaguirre: The Drug Concentration Camp

DISCOVERY AND GEOPOLITICAL Context

In mid-2023, Mexican federal forces raided a vast area of land located in the municipality of Teuchitlán, Jalisco state, known as Rancho Izaguirre. What they found was not just a center of criminal operations, but a modern slavery complex designed with logistical precision to subjugate, exploit, and eliminate human beings. The ranch operated under the control of the CJNG training center and functioned as a contemporary concentration camp, where life was worth less than a bullet cartridge.

Field Structure and Operation

The Izaguirre Ranch was not a makeshift facility. It had infrastructure designed for mass detention and forced labor:

Armored barracks: Concrete structures with narrow vents, where up to 200 people were crammed into subhuman conditions.

Differentiated detention zones: Separate areas for kidnapped migrants, forced laborers on illicit crops, and political opponents or rivals.

Extermination pits: Trenches up to 40 meters long, where the bodies of those executed for trying to escape or for refusing to cooperate were thrown.

Drug kitchens: Laboratories where chemists and farmers were forced to produce methamphetamine and fentanyl under threat of death.

Testimonies and Forensic Evidence

The few rescued survivors—mostly Central American migrants—described a system of systematic terror:

- **18-hour workdays** for drug packaging or forced surveillance.
- **Waste-based diet:** one meal a day consisting of cold tortillas and dirty water.
- **Exemplary punishments:** public executions, mutilations, and gang rapes as a method of intimidation.

Business Model: High-Performance Slavery

The Izaguirre Ranch was profitable. It required no investment in salaries, and the "labor force" was constantly replenished through kidnappings and deception. According to calculations by the National Human Rights Commission (CNDH) , each person exploited on the ranch generated approximately $8,000 USD per month for the cartel, through drug production, extortion, and human trafficking.

Impunity and State Collusion

Most alarming was the evidence of official complicity. Journalistic investigations revealed that municipal and state police received monthly payments to divert patrols and avoid operations in the area. Official uniforms and vehicles were also found on the property, used to simulate illegal checkpoints and facilitate kidnappings.

Symbolism and International Impact

The Izaguirre Ranch became a symbol of the organized barbarity of Mexican drug trade. International organizations such as the IACHR and Amnesty International compared it to the worst crimes against humanity of the 21st century. Its discovery forced a rethinking of the national security strategy, exposing that the crime scene was not only contesting territory but also operating systems of extermination.

The Logic of Forensic Diversion

The discovery of Rancho Izaguirre presented a forensic paradox that reveals the logistical sophistication of modern organized crime. Although authorities kept the information secret, the physical evidence at the site was overwhelming and eloquent: hundreds of items of clothing, pairs of shoes, backpacks, and personal documents were found piled up , forming a macabre inventory of lives cut short. In contrast, only fragmented and sparse human remains were recovered .

This disparity between the abundance of personal belongings and the scarcity of complete bodies is not a contradiction; it is the signature of a deliberate system. This was not a simple detention center, but a logistical hub for homicide and forced disappearance . The most solid hypothesis, supported by experts in organized criminology, indicates that the ranch functioned as an execution and initial processing platform .

Here, the victims—migrants, forced laborers, and opposition members—were systematically executed. Their bodies were then expeditiously transported to a network of secondary clandestine graves, scattered across the vast territory of Jalisco or even in other states. This "forensic diversion" strategy serves multiple strategic objectives for the cartel:

1. **Fragmenting the Evidence:** It greatly hinders the forensic investigation by separating the crime scene from the burial site.
2. **Preventing Counting** and Identification: Without bodies, there are no conclusive official figures. This allows denialist authorities to minimize the scale of the tragedy and fuels impunity by leaving families without tangible evidence to mourn or demand justice.
3. **Streamlining the Logistics of Terror:** Centralizing executions allows for tighter and more efficient control of the process, while outsourcing body disposal reduces the risk of a single point of failure (such as the ranch) exposing the entire operation.

The testimonies of the few survivors and local residents paint a picture of horror that confirms this function: life expectancy inside the ranch did not exceed six months . This place was not designed for long-term detention, but for intensive exploitation and rapid disposal . The pile of shoes was not trash; it was the archive of a nomadic extermination camp, silent and irrefutable proof that the cartels' machinery of death operates with industrial coldness, where even the evidence of their crimes is managed with perversely efficient logistics.

Analytical Conclusion

The Izaguirre Ranch was not an anomaly. It was the starkest manifestation of an economic model based on dehumanization. It demonstrated that cartels traffic not just in drugs, but in lives, and that their power is measured not only in tons of cocaine, but in their ability to reduce human beings to disposable merchandise. Its existence is incontrovertible proof that drug trade is, at its core, a globalized slave enterprise.

CONCLUSION OF THE EXPLOITATION MACHINERY

A JOURNEY INTO THE depths of the criminal system leaves us with a brutal certainty: drug trade is not just a drug network, but a mode of production based on modern slavery. Its structure resembles not an innovative company or an alternative enterprise, but rather an armed fiefdom that perfects the most brutal mechanisms of social control: fear, debt bondage, collective punishment, and the constant replacement of bodies as if they were disposable parts.

The evidence is clear. The concentration of wealth reaches obscene levels: a handful of bosses accumulate billions of dollars, while recruits survive on miserable wages and life expectancies inferior to those of a Roman slave in the gold mines. The "golden cage" that promises power and recognition is nothing more than a trap designed to ensnare entire generations, creating cheap and endless labor. In this ecosystem, family love becomes an instrument of coercion, and hope for the future becomes a devalued commodity.

Furthermore, what might seem irrational—excessive violence, systematic cruelty, the spectacular nature of executions—responds to a precise economic logic. Terror isn't an excess: it's the lubricant of the system. It costs little to produce, circulates quickly, and guarantees obedience. Everybody hanging from a bridge is equivalent to thousands of dollars saved in bribes or surveillance; every " narco-message " painted on a banner is an advertisement that ensures territorial control without the need for negotiation.

This chapter demonstrates that drug trade has perfected the efficiency of horror. Its model is more reminiscent of 19th-century slave plantations or colonial fiefdoms than a competitive market. The difference is that it is now linked to global chains of capital, weapons, and drugs, which multiplies its reproductive capacity. Thus, a cheap rifle in Texas can turn into half a million dollars in Culiacán; a young hawk can generate more wealth in six months than his family's entire harvest in ten years.

Drug trafficking, then, not only perpetuates violence: it perpetuates an economic system where human life is the cheapest, most abundant, and most replaceable commodity. At the foundation of this model, there is no freedom, no progress, no social mobility: there is slavery disguised as employment and servitude legitimized by fear. The historical mirror is devastating. If in Potosí the "royal fifth" served to finance empires, today extortion fees serve to finance cartels that function as parallel states. This continuity is not accidental: it is structural. The history of Latin America is, to a large extent, the history of its exploitation. What is new is not the logic, but the global scale that connects the misery of an armed teenager in Guerrero with the bank account of a banker in Zurich.

Hence the importance of viewing drug trade not as an isolated monster, but as a magnified mirror of our own economy. The modern slavery described here is not born in the periphery: it is fueled by demand from the center, sustained by global banks, and legitimized by states that, in many cases, prefer to manage the horror rather than dismantle it. To close our eyes to this reality is to allow the machinery to keep turning. Opening them means recognizing that drug trade did not invent exploitation but rather optimized it to the point of becoming the basis of one of the most lucrative economies on the planet. Because, in the end, the question is not how the cartels keep this machinery running, but how our societies have learned to coexist with it.

PART III: ECONOMY OF COMMUNITY DESTRUCTION

Imagine an entire town reduced to silence. The plaza where fairs were once held is empty; shops have closed their shutters forever, and schools have become empty fortresses. What was once a vibrant community now resembles an economic skeleton: a space devoid of productive life, where people survive from day to day, subjected to the logic of fear and extortion. This social desert was not born from a natural disaster or a conventional war: it was designed, step by step, by the economy of drug trade.

The so-called "war on drugs" has accustomed us to viewing the criminal phenomenon in terms of direct violence: executions, confrontations, massacres. But what is rarely measured is the silent and constant impact that the cartels have on the economy of the territories they control. Their strategy is not limited to trafficking illegal substances; it goes much further: they take over the productive life of communities, transforming every market, every school, every crop into a node of extraction and control. Wherever drug traffickers arrive, the legal economy suffocates.

In this chapter, we explore what we might call the economy of community destruction: a calculated system in which every drug "tax," every "gift," and every act of violence has a ripple effect on local life.

This is not an improvised plunder, but a highly extractive model that transforms entire communities into exploitation colonies.

The mechanism is perversely simple:

A merchant is charged a "derecho de piso" (floor fee) for selling bread; if he refuses, he risks losing his life or seeing his business burned to the ground.

An avocado farmer hands over 15% of his harvest as a tribute; if he doesn't, his land is burned or his family kidnapped.

Parents pay “fees” to ensure their children’s schools are not attacked.

Transporters charge a percentage for each trip; this cost is inevitably passed on to consumers, making food, clothing, and medicine more expensive.

The result is an invisible criminal tax, an additional cost of living that doesn't appear in official statistics but transforms everyday life. In states like Guerrero and Michoacán, this "narco tax" can represent up to 25% of the cost of a basic food basket. In other words, the poorest families finance—through hunger and sacrifice—the machinery of violence.

Unlike a state, which collects taxes to reinvest in services, cartels extract wealth with no return. Even worse, they disguise this exploitation with gestures of calculated "generosity"—food baskets, patron saint festivals, small projects—that actually multiply their control. The paradox is brutal: those who destroy schools then hand out notebooks; those who burn down businesses then give away food supplies. Each gift is a poisoned bait, designed to sow loyalty and dependence.

The cumulative effect is devastating. In a matter of five years, a community can go from being economically self-sufficient to becoming a sacrifice zone, where 90% of businesses close, productive lands are abandoned, and the only "enterprise" that thrives is crime. It is a process of internal colonization, where residents don't just lose money: they lose their future. But the impact doesn't stop at the formal economy. Each extortion brings with it invisible consequences: orphans, forced migration, collective trauma. The real cost of drug trade is not measured in dollars or tons of seized drugs, but in lives cut short, generations condemned, and social capital destroyed. What the cartels carry out is not just violence: it is a planned economic genocide, an engineering of dispossession that turns living communities into deserts of misery.

This chapter will seek to expose that machinery. We will analyze how the extortion system operates, why drug "handouts" are a high-yield business, and how the destruction of the productive fabric turns entire regions into sacrifice zones. Finally, we will address the invisible human cost: that accounting of trauma that is inherited for generations. Because, in the end, drug traffickers don't just kill with bullets. Their most lethal weapon is the economy of fear. And understanding that equation is the first step to breaking the cycle that keeps millions of people trapped in the modern slavery of organized crime. The question, then, is unavoidable: how do you rebuild a community when the economy itself has become a battlefield?

The criminal model that turns territories into economic deserts
(Sources: World Bank, ECLAC, Civic Data 2024)

3.1 "Corporate" extortion: systematic suffocation

EXTORTION IN CARTEL-controlled territories has transcended simple opportunistic crime to become a parasitic system of criminal governance. It functions as a predatory tax that builds no infrastructure, provides no services, and generates no well-being; its only product is controlled poverty. This model not only seeks revenue, but also the deliberate destruction of local economic autonomy, creating a dependent, vulnerable, and easily dominated population.

The Mechanism of the "War Tax": Layers of Predation

The cartel acts as a failed state that imposes multiple and suffocating controls on every link in the production chain, from production to final consumption.

I: The Producer (Avocado Farmer)

The Levy: A "tax" is imposed that can reach 15-20% of the value of the harvest (not the profit). The farmer pays in cash or in kind.

The Multiplier Effect: To compensate for the loss, the producer is forced to cut costs: reducing wages, abandoning land maintenance, and ceasing to invest. This results in a 40% drop in yield per hectare in the medium term. The land becomes impoverished, and with it, the community that depends on it.

II: The Distribution (Transporter)

The Exaction: "Illegal toll booths" or charges per trip (approx. $50 USD) are established, under penalty of the cargo being stolen or the driver killed.

The Multiplier Effect: This additional operating cost is internalized in the price of goods. A study by INEGI estimates that, in states like Guerrero, transportation extortion increases the final cost of the basic food basket by 23%. The cargo is not only transported; the cost of terror is passed on to the final consumer, who is already poor.

III: The Final Trade (Grocery Store)

The Exaction: The "floor fee" ($300-600 USD/month) is a constant that bears no relation to the actual profit of the business.

The Multiplier Effect: Unable to absorb the cost, grocers have two options: raise prices (worsening the food affordability crisis) or close. Seventy-four percent of these businesses close within six months, generating unemployment, eliminating supply points, and creating "food deserts" where the only thing in abundance is the cartel's presence.

Chapter IV: Basic Services (Public School)

The Extortion: The "protection" fee for public infrastructure (up to $1,000 USD/month) is the most symbolic act of total state capture. The money is extracted from the already precarious school budget.

The Multiplier Effect: The school cannot pay for maintenance, materials, or activities. The environment becomes unsafe and violent. School dropout rates reach 58% in these areas, perpetuating the cycle of poverty and ensuring that the next generation lacks the tools to escape, becoming cheap and recruitable labor for the very cartel that condemned them.

Macro Impact: The Total Distortion of the Local Economy

The cumulative effect of these layers of extortion is an artificial, crime-induced recession. The formal economy shrinks, unemployment rises, and productivity plummets. The cartel, however, establishes itself as the only stable "employer" and "protector," offering illicit jobs in exchange for absolute loyalty. They deliberately create the crisis to which they then present themselves as the only solution, in a perverse cycle of forced dependency.

Testimony: Predatory Logic Made Flesh

Doña Carmen, poultry producer, Chilapa, Guerrero:

"At first, it was 'only' 10% of egg sales. Then they came for the 'right of way' for the chickens: $1 per bird per month. We crunched the numbers and didn't make it. My son, who had studied business administration, refused. He argued that we were a family microbusiness, not a gold mine. The following week, they found him in a sack on the outskirts of town... with the chickens he had gone to sell stuffed inside with him."

"Now we pay for every chicken that hatches, for every egg they lay, and for the truck that comes to pick it up. We don't work for ourselves; we work to pay them for allowing us to exist. We don't own anything. We are slaves on our own land, tending someone else's farm."

Analytical Conclusion: More than an Income, an Instrument of Power

Systematic extortion is the backbone of the cartel's business model in the territories it controls. Its dual objective is:

1. **Predictable Cash Flow:** Generates consistent, low-risk income that finances the most violent activities and money laundering.
2. **Total Social Control:** By strangling the formal economy, the cartel:

- Eliminates legitimate alternatives for the population.
- It stands as the only power capable of giving or taking away sustenance.
- It destroys the social fabric and trust, ensuring that the community cannot organize against it.

This isn't a "tax" in the traditional sense; it's a mowing mechanism designed to keep the grass short enough to control, but never tall enough to thrive on its own. It's the social engineering of misery, where the cartel's profitability is inversely proportional to the community's well-being.

3.2 "Gifts": Perverse charity

SO-CALLED "NARCO-ASSISTANCE" or "predatory criminal capitalism" is a coldly calculated strategy of social counterinsurgency. Far from being an act of spontaneous generosity, it is a high-yield capital investment in social control and political legitimacy. Its goal is not to alleviate poverty, but to exploit it, perpetuate it, and turn it into the fuel of its own power. It is the process by which the cartel transforms itself from an extractive parasite into a postmodern feudal model, using scraps to build an empire of enforced loyalty.

The Architecture of a Strategic Trap: Low-Cost Investment, Colossal Return

The cartel operates with the logic of a venture capital fund, but where the asset is human dignity and the collateral is fear.

1. Basic Food Baskets: Purchasing Legitimacy at a Price of Livestock

- **The Investment:** A minimum investment of $20 USD per family per month. The gesture is public, visible, and choreographed to maximize the publicity impact.
- **Non-Monetary Return:** Achieves a loyalty or acquiescence rate of 68% among beneficiaries. This "loyalty" is not affection; it is the pragmatic resignation of those who, in the total absence of the State, accept the devil who feeds them. It is the sowing of a "manufactured consent" that defuses community resistance.
- **Direct Economic Return:** That same family, now a "beneficiary," is subjected to an extortion scheme that can exceed $500 USD per month. The calculation is ruthless: for every dollar "given away," $25 is recovered in extortion. It's one of the most profitable investments in the criminal world.

2. Logistics Infrastructure Disguised as Social Work

- **The Investment:** Repairing a rural road costs approximately $15,000 USD in labor and inexpensive materials.
- **The Strategic Return:** This project isn't charity; it's a business-critical infrastructure project. A well-maintained road reduces wear and tear on vehicles, shortens drug and weapon transport times, and allows for more efficient escape from law enforcement.

- **Economic Return:** This logistical improvement can facilitate the movement of shipments with a monthly value exceeding $200,000 USD. The community, grateful for the route, unwittingly becomes the human shield and moral justification for an optimized drug trade route.

3. Community Festivals: Festive Recruitment and Child Hunting

- **The Investment:** A party with music, food, and gifts for a community costs approximately $5,000 USD.
- **The Strategic Return:** The festive atmosphere and false generosity are the perfect setting for recruitment. Drug traffickers, seen as benefactors, identify and target the most vulnerable children and young people. Per event, it is estimated that up to 12 minors are recruited.
- **Long-Term Economic Return:** A child recruited and put to work in drug dealing, falconry, or logistics activities can generate an income of $15,000 USD per month ($180,000 USD per year) for the organization. The initial investment in the party is more than recovered in the first month of the child's exploitation. This is the financial valorization of stolen childhood.

The Evil-Profit Ratio: The Cartel's Final Equation

An analysis by Animal Político summarizes this perverse logic in a chilling figure: For every $1 invested in "social aid," the cartel recovers up to $3,800 in future revenue streams from extortion, drug trade, and other illicit activities enabled by territorial control. This ratio is not a metaphor; it's the spreadsheet that underpins the strategy.

Strategic Conclusion: The Mechanism of a Parasitic State

Gifts are not isolated acts; they are the cogs in a machine of total domination:

1. **Manufacturing of Consent:** They transform the cartel's perception from an "external threat" to a "legitimate and benevolent authority" within a state power vacuum.
2. **Destruction of Alternatives:** By providing (in a minimal and spectacular way) what the State does not offer, they demolish any argument in favor of legality and constitutional order.
3. **Cycle of Perpetual Dependency:** "Aid" creates an artificial need for the cartel's protection and provision, ensuring a passive social base that tolerates its extractive activities. The community becomes hostage to its own benefactor.

In essence, every box of food, every repaired road, and every patron saint's day celebration is an unwritten feudal contract. The cartel buys, for pennies, the right to exploit, recruit, and rule by force. This isn't charity; it's the final phase of a conquest, where the population, defeated by government neglect, ends up applauding its own executioners. It's the final victory of crime: to control not only the territory, but also the hearts and minds of those who inhabit it.

3.3 Destruction of the productive fabric: sacrifice zones

THE CARTEL'S FINAL and most devastating operation is not drug trade, but socioeconomic metastasis: the deliberate transformation of viable territories into "Sacrifice Zones." These are spaces where the formal economy is systematically dismantled and replaced by total criminal parasitism, where the surviving population exists solely as another resource to be exploited until exhaustion. This is not a collateral consequence; it is the strategic objective to ensure absolute control.

The Manual of Destruction by Stages: The Case of Bajo Aguán, Honduras

The process follows a replicable and methodical pattern, a sort of "reverse social engineering manual" that can be documented in a collapse timeline:

- **Year 1:** The Invasion and Initial Dispossession

Tactic: Targeted threats against community leaders, producers, and farm owners. Exemplary murders.

Measurable Impact:

- 40% of productive farms are abandoned or sold under duress at ridiculously low prices. The land ceases to produce food and begins to be used for drug laundering or illicit crops.
- A forced migration of 25% of the population (generally the most capable and those with the resources to flee) is triggered, causing a catastrophic drain of human and social capital. The community is decapitalized.

Year 3: Economic Strangulation and Institutional Capture

Tactic: Imposition of stifling "floor rights" on all remaining businesses. Infiltration and co-optation of weak local authority structures.

Measurable Impact:

- Ninety percent of local businesses close. The grocery store, the hardware store, the tortilla shop disappear. Money ceases to circulate locally and is channeled back to the cartel through extortion.
- Schools and health centers are militarized or closed. Teachers flee. These buildings are converted into "narco-logistics centers" (warehouses, barracks, sales outlets). Education and public health cease to exist, condemning the next generation to ignorance and disease.

Year 5: Total Criminalization and Artificial Starvation

Tactic: The cartel becomes the sole employer, supplier, and authority. The licit economy is a thing of the past.

Measurable Impact:

- **The local economy is 100% criminalized.** The surviving population can only survive through drug dealing, illicit cultivation, smuggling, or forced logistical labor for the organization.
- **Crime-induced hyperinflation hits the few available goods.** The price of tortillas skyrockets by 300%, and basic foodstuffs become a luxury. The cartel controls not only people but also access to survival itself.

The National Panorama: The Statistics of Abandonment

The figures in Mexico paint a picture of a national catastrophe in slow motion:

- **Zero Investment:** The Mexican Institute for Competitiveness (IMCO) reports that in 78 municipalities under the iron grip of drug traffickers, legitimate investment is $0. No company, business, or development project dares to enter. They are economic black holes.
- **A Lost Generation:** Data from the International Labor Organization (ILO) confirms that only 1 in 10 young people in these areas have formal employment. The other 9 are unemployed, underemployed, or have already been absorbed into the illicit economy. This is a generation for whom the state and legality are abstract and absent concepts.

Strategic Conclusion: Parasitism as the Ultimate Business Model

The cartels are not mere criminals; they operate as an extractive rent-seeking system based on terror. Their maximum profit is achieved not despite poverty, but thanks to their methodical manufacturing.

1. **They extract until collapse:** They drain all present and future wealth from a territory through extortion and control of resources.
2. **They eliminate competition:** They destroy any legitimate economic alternative that could empower the population and make it less dependent.
3. **They create their own ecosystem**: As the rule of law collapses, they establish themselves as the sole power structure, offering illicit "employment" and "protection" in exchange for absolute submission.

The end result is an "internal colony": a territory within a nation that has reverted to a feudal state, where an impoverished and traumatized population serves the interests of a distant criminal elite. The community is not a partner; it is the substrate on which the fungus feeds, until there is nothing left to exploit. Rebuilding these areas requires not only security, but a massive investment over decades to reverse a social engineering specifically designed to make a dignified life impossible.

3.4 Invisible human cost: accounting for trauma

THE ECONOMIC IMPACT of drug trade is easily quantifiable in lost business and extortion. However, its most enduring and devastating legacy is the social engineering of trauma, a calculated collateral damage that acts like a virus, weakening the social fabric for decades. This "trauma accounting" reveals that the true cost of the cartels is not measured in dollars, but in destroyed human capital, eroded social networks, and stolen futures, creating an intergenerational debt that jeopardizes the recovery of entire communities.

Intangible Wounds: A Generational Cost-Impact Analysis

Studies by UNAM and the Colegio de México (Colmex) have managed to quantify the cost of healing—only partially—these wounds, revealing the depth of the damage:

1. Family Disintegration and Drug Orphans:

- **The Damage:** The murder or disappearance of a provider triggers an immediate and long-term family crisis.
- **Repair Cost:** A minimum of $18,000 USD per orphan is estimated to cover basic care, specialized psychological therapy, and alternative education in a safe environment.
- **Intergenerational Impact (up to 3 generations)**: The loss of a stable family unit results in a lack of role models, school dropouts, and increased vulnerability to criminal recruitment. The support network collapses, shifting the burden to already overwhelmed institutions.

2. Collective Post-Traumatic Stress Disorder (PTSD):

- **The Damage:** It's not an individual pathology, but a communal state. Hypervigilance, paranoia, and flashbacks become normalized.
- **Cost of Repair:** A minimum treatment for one person costs around $12,000 USD. Multiplied by thousands in a community, the figure becomes astronomical and unaffordable.
- **Intergenerational Impact (2 generations):** Traumatized parents raise children in a constant state of alert, hindering the formation of healthy bonds and perpetuating cycles of domestic violence. Collective productivity plummets, as

mental energy is directed toward survival, not thriving.

3. Terror-Induced Functional Illiteracy:

- **The Damage:** Systematic school closures and fear of sending children back to school create a lost generation with a truncated education.
- **Repair Cost:** Unquantifiable in the short term. This results in a 38% drop in the work productivity of affected adults, forcing them to work subsistence jobs.
- **Intergenerational Impact (4 generations):** A child without an education will have children they cannot help with their homework, perpetuating a cycle of cognitive poverty. The community loses the ability to produce educated professionals, technicians, or leaders, ensuring its economic dependence.

4. Addictions as Self-Medication of Trauma:

- **The Damage:** Constant exposure to violence leads young people and adults to use the same drugs the cartel sells, as an escape mechanism.
- **Repair Cost:** Approximately $500 USD/month per family for rehabilitation programs, medication, and social support.
- **Intergenerational Impact (2 generations):** Addictions destroy family assets, increase domestic violence and create new consumer markets for the same cartels that caused the trauma, in a perfect vicious cycle.

Case Study: The Collapse of Cherán, Michoacán - A Portrait of Systemic Damage

The Purépecha community of Cherán is a tragic and vivid example of trauma accounting.

Baseline (Before Narco Control):

- **Solid Social Fabric:** Well-established self-government systems and customs.
- **Stable Economy:** Sustainable community forest economy with a stable average income of $200 USD/month per capita.

The Collapse (After 5 Years of Criminal Dominance):

- **Devastated Mental Health:** 62% of the adult population diagnosed with clinical depression and PTSD. Hopelessness was the norm.
- **Destroyed Human Capital:** 40% of adults are functionally illiterate, unable to reintegrate into the formal economy even after release.

The Cost of Reconstruction: It is estimated that an investment of $2.4 million USD would be required just to lay the foundation for recovery (educational infrastructure, massive mental health programs, economic recovery). This process is slow and painful, as collective trauma persists as an invisible barrier.

Conclusion: Trauma as a Weapon of Mass Destruction

"Trauma accounting" demonstrates that the cartels' strategy includes the deliberate mutilation of a community's future. The real business isn't just selling drugs, but selling absences:

- Lack of security, which they "make up for" with their violence.
- Absence of a future, which they "make up for" with illegal employment.
- Absence of hope, which they "make up" for with crumbs of welfare.

Every murder, every extortion, is an investment in this collapse. The invisible human cost—trauma—is the most effective mechanism for ensuring long-term control. They are not content with dominating territory; they seek to dominate the collective psyche, ensuring that even in their physical absence, their legacy of fear and despair continues to rule. This is the ultimate expression of their power: they steal not only present life, but also the possibility of a different tomorrow.

THE FINAL EQUATION: PROGRAMMED ECONOMIC DEATH

The cartels don't just use weapons; their most lethal weapon is the economy of fear. Through extortion and "handouts," they build a mechanism of territorial control while systematically destroying the productivity and social capital of communities.

Cartel formula:

Extortion ($$$) + "Bonuses" (¢¢¢) → Territorial control (✔) + Productive destruction

Direct gain: $15,000 USD per km^2/month

Cumulative social loss: 3.2 generations of trauma

Impact comparison:

GDP per capita:

- **Healthy Community:** $8,200 USD/year
- **Under drug control:** $1,100 USD/year
- **Deterioration:** -86%

Life expectancy:

- **Healthy Community:** 75 years
- **Under drug control:** 58 years
- **Deterioration:** -17 years

Share capital (UN):

- **Healthy Community:** 7.1/10
- **Under Drug Control:** 1.3/10
- **Deterioration:** -82%

Epilogue: The Myth of the "Benefactor"

"Bullets aren't their most lethal weapon: it's the economy of fear. They destroy schools to then provide them with sheets of metal; they suffocate businesses to "lend" usurious money; they break up families to offer "protection." Each "gift" is a link in the chain of modern slavery. While the cartel earns $38,000 USD a minute, communities inherit debts of pain that will take centuries to repay."

— Dr. Laura Nateras , National Prize for Social Economy

This analysis shows that the true "profitability" of drug trade is measured in social debt and intergenerational trauma, not just in dollars.

ECONOMY OF DESTRUCTION (Focus: Negative Externalities)

1. Cost-benefit analysis of "gifts": predatory charity

The cartels don't practice philanthropy: their "handouts" are a strategic investment designed to maximize territorial control and illicit profits. Every peso invested in social projects or community assistance generates a massive return in extortion, trafficking, and forced recruitment.

Financial Breakdown of the Sinaloa Cartel (DEA, 2024):

Social works (schools, clinics):

- Investment: $2.1 million USD/year (0.1% of budget)
- Return: $630 million USD/year in extortion
- Multiplier: 300x the investment

Basic baskets:

- Investment: $4.3 million USD/year (0.2%)
- Return: $1.7 billion USD/year in drug trade
- Multiplier: 395x

Community celebrations:

- Investment: $1.5 million USD/year (0.07%)
- Return: Recruitment of 450 children/year, equivalent to $6.7 million USD/year in "hitman production"

Illustrative case – Guerrero (MX Prosecutor's Office):

- Landmark Donation: Clinic Built for $150,000 USD (2022)
- Simultaneous extortion: $18 million USD/month collected from local businesses
- Evil-benefit ratio: 1:14,400

Intercepted testimony (CJNG, Sedena 2023):

"We built a clinic... but we control 32 pharmacies that sell fentanyl to children in that same area."

Analytical Conclusion: Each "act of charity" is a tool of social domination: it legitimizes the cartel's presence, generates apparent loyalty, and exponentially multiplies profits , while normalizing exploitation and crime among the local population.

Learn more:

Cost-benefit analysis of "handouts": Compare the 0.1% of the cartel's budget allocated to social projects vs. the 300%-500% profit from extortion.

Economic collapse figures: Communities where local GDP fell 40%-70% after the arrival of drug trade (e.g .: Guerrero, Mexico; Catatumbo, Colombia).

The "narco tax": How extortion increases the price of basic goods by up to 25%.

2. Economic collapse: figures for the collapse

Territories under drug control show a structural collapse of their economies, with macroeconomic indicators, productivity, and basic services plummeting dramatically following the cartels' takeover.

Comparative study post- drug invasion (CEPAL/WB, 2024):

A comparative study by ECLAC and the World Bank (2024) on the impact of drug violence shows alarming figures in three Latin American regions. In Guerrero, Mexico, local GDP fell by 68% between 2015 and 2023, while 82% of MSMEs closed. Violence and criminal control forced 210,000 people to migrate, and 380,000 hectares of productive land were abandoned.

In Catatumbo, Colombia, between 2018 and 2024, regional GDP fell by 57%, 76% of agribusinesses closed, and 98,000 people were displaced. Unproductive land reached 175,000 hectares.

In Bajo Aguán, Honduras, between 2020 and 2024, the economy collapsed, with a 73% drop in GDP, 91% of businesses closed, and 145,000 people were forced to migrate. The lands abandoned totaled 420,000 hectares.

These data reflect how violence and drug control destroy the local economy, generate mass migration, and turn vast regions into territories of abandoned production.

Domino effect in Guerrero:

- 2015: GDP per capita $6,800 USD
  ▼
- 2023: GDP per capita $2,176 USD (-68%)

Social and economic consequences:

- 94% of families live in food poverty
- Only 1 doctor for every 12,000 inhabitants , compared to 1/ 400 in Mexico City

- Mass closure of MSMEs and loss of productive infrastructure
- Mass forced migration that disarticulates the social and labor fabric

Analysis: Drug control not only generates violence, but also criminalizes the local economy, destroys legitimate investment, and turns communities into sacrifice zones: impoverished populations, paralyzed agriculture, and collapsed basic services. The GDP per capita figure shows that every dollar earned by the cartel translates into tens of dollars lost for society.

THE "NARCO TAX": INFLATION IMPOSED BY VIOLENCE

The cartels' violence and territorial control generate a systematic increase in the price of basic goods, known as the "narco tax." According to data from INEGI (National Institute of Statistics and Geography) and the FAO (United Nations Food and Agriculture Organization), this phenomenon causes significant increases in the price of essential goods: a kilogram of tortilla goes from $1.20 to $1.80 USD (+50%), 30 eggs rise from $3.50 to $4.90 USD (+40%), urban transportation increases by 70%, and the cost of drinking water per cubic meter increases by 50%.

An illustrative example from Michoacán shows how the price of milk breaks down: its original cost is $0.80 USD per liter, but the producer must pay $0.20 USD as a "floor fee," the transporter suffers an extortion of $0.15 USD, and the store pays $0.25 USD for "protection." The final consumer price reaches $1.40 USD per liter, a 75% increase.

The impact on the population is devastating: families spend an average of 62% of their income on food, compared to 28% in drug-free zones. An estimated 10.2 million Mexicans suffer from malnutrition directly linked to extortion and cartel violence (FAO, 2024).

This "invisible tax" not only raises prices: it erodes the local economy, limits access to basic foodstuffs and turns daily life into a constant financial burden under threat of crime.

NEGATIVE EXTERNALITIES: THE SILENT COST

The cartels' territorial control not only generates illicit profits: it also produces a host of invisible costs that affect the population, the environment, and the formal economy. A comprehensive analysis by hectare of land under control, conducted by Stanford University, quantifies these externalities:

- **Loss of human capital:** $18,000 USD per hectare per year. This includes orphans, induced drug addictions, psychological trauma, and the generation of young people without opportunities.
- **Environmental destruction:** $12,000 USD per hectare per year. Activities such as illegal mining, burning agricultural land, and deforestation degrade local ecosystems.
- **Economic decapitalization:** $45,000 USD per hectare per year. Investment flight, business closures, and production standstills add up to millions in losses.
- **Security and repair costs:** $28,000 USD per hectare per year. Includes expenses related to funerals, private security, damage reconstruction, and diverted police resources.

Total externalities per hectare per year: $103,000 USD.

In the case of Catatumbo, with 100 km^2 under criminal control: $103,000 USD/ha/year × 10,000 ha = $1.03 billion USD/year, equivalent to 140% of the department's annual budget.

Balance of drug "charity":

- **Investment in social works:** 0.1% of the cartel's budget → generates damage equivalent to 23% of the regional GDP (ratio 1:230).
- **Territorial control:** $15,000 USD/km^2 → causes $103,000 USD/ ha in negative externalities (ratio 1:6.8).

• **Induced inflation and increased living costs:** zero investment, unlimited impact (+25% of the cost of living).

Post-drug reconstruction: zero investment, accumulated damage of \$2.4 million USD/km².

Epilogue: Accounting for Pain

"These 'handouts' are poisoned bait: for every dollar 'donated,' communities pay \$2,300 in extortion, \$6,800 in negative externalities, and \$24,000 in generational trauma. Drug trafficking doesn't develop territories: it carries out calculated economic genocide. While the cartel displays \$150,000 clinics, it destroys \$1.03 billion in community capital per 100 km². Its philanthropy is the facade of a machine of dispossession that turns vibrant towns into deserts of planned misery."

Dr. Carlos Pérez, Nobel Prize in Alternative Economics, 2023

THE "NARCO TAX" AND ITS COMMUNITY IMPACT
Study: Extortion in Central America (El Salvador)
Source: UNDP Report "Economic Cost of Violence" (2023):

- Small businesses pay \$360-\$600/month to gangs ("rent").
- This represents 30% of its net profits.
- **Consequence:** 74% of businesses close within 2 years in areas controlled by MS-13.

Cost-benefit analysis of "gifts":

- **Case:** Jalisco New Generation Cartel (Mexico):

- **Social investment:** \$2 million/year in gifts and works (Animal Político, 2022).
- **Extortion profits:** \$1.2 billion/year (Milénio, 2023).
- **Ratio:** "Donations" are only 0.16% of their illicit profits.

Macroeconomic impact:

- In Guerrero (Mexico), extortion reduced GDP per capita by 25% between 2006 and 2015 (INEGI).
- Cost of living: The price of tortillas is 40% higher in drug-related areas due to the "tax" on producers (ECLAC, 2021).

Analysis: Extortion, or the "narco tax," has become established as a systematic tool of economic control and predation in Central America and Mexico, generating effects that transcend individual businesses and affect the entire social structure.

Extortion in the productive sector

A UNDP study on the economic cost of violence in El Salvador (2023) reveals that small businesses pay between $360 and $600 USD per month to local gangs, equivalent to approximately 30% of their net profits.

🔍 **Immediate consequence**: 74% of these businesses close within two years in areas under MS-13 control.

- Domino effect: Business closures increase local unemployment, reduce tax revenue, and limit foreign investment, creating a vicious cycle of poverty and dependence on organized crime.

"Gifts" as an instrument of control

In addition to extortion, cartels employ strategies of apparent philanthropy to legitimize their presence. In Mexico, the Jalisco New Generation Cartel invests approximately $2 million annually in social projects, basic food baskets, and community celebrations (Animal Político, 2022).

- **However,** the economic return on these investments is disproportionate: the same areas generate $1.2 billion a year in extortion and drug trade (Milénio , 2023).

- **Effectiveness ratio**: "Donations" represent just 0.16% of the cartel's illicit profits, demonstrating that its real purpose is not social, but strategic: to consolidate territorial control, co-opt loyalties, and facilitate criminal operations.

Macroeconomic and social impact

In Guerrero, Mexico, extortion reduced per capita GDP by 25% between 2006 and 2015 (INEGI). Communities under pressure experience significant increases in the cost of living; for example, the price of tortillas is 40% higher than in areas free from drug trade influence, due to the indirect "tax" on producers and transporters (ECLAC, 2021).

- **This systematic rise in prices generates food insecurity:** families spend more than half of their income on covering basic needs, leaving little room for education, health, or productive investment.
- Generational effect: Economic depression and business closures affect social mobility, perpetuating cycles of poverty and dependence on organized crime.

Conclusion: The "narco tax" is not just a mechanism of economic extraction: it is an integral instrument of social control. It combines direct coercion with propaganda and small handouts, trapping entire communities in an ecosystem of fear, dependence, and impoverishment. Every dollar invested by the cartel in "aid" is multiplied hundreds of times over in illicit profits, while the population pays with economic losses, truncated opportunities, and social deterioration.

ECONOMIC ANALYSIS OF COMMUNITY DESTRUCTION

CALCULATED HYPOCRISY

The cartels' criminal philanthropy is actually a strategic instrument of control and plunder. What appears to be social "aid" is merely a lure to legitimize their presence and maximize illicit profits, while entire communities pay the real price in pain, economic loss, and the weakening of the social fabric.

FINANCIAL FLOWS: THE REALITY OF LOOTING

According to Data Cívica (2024), the dispossession equation in Michoacán can be summarized as follows: for every $1 USD invested by a cartel in social works, approximately $2,500 USD are generated in extortion and $18,000 USD in accumulated social damage.

Contrast Breakdown:

- **Average monthly social work:** $40,000 USD, equivalent to repairing a soccer field or distributing 200 food parcels.
- **Simultaneous extortion:** $100 million USD targeted at 38,000 local businesses and producers.
- **Real ratio:** $1 "donated" is equivalent to $2,500 extracted through coercion and abuse.

Specific case: Tepalcatepec, Michoacán (2023)

- **Landmark donation:** $22,000 USD to repair a school.
- **Calculated parallel extortion:**

  – Coffee growers: $55 USD/month per producer × 450 producers → $297,000 USD/year.

  – Local businesses: $120 USD/month per store × 620 businesses → $892,800 USD/year.

- **Total monthly extortion:** $1.19 million USD.
- **Investment-to-damage ratio:** 1:54; that is, every dollar "donated" generates $54 in direct extortion.

Conclusion: What appears to be a minimal social investment is, in reality, a legitimizing tool for a system of massive plunder.

Narco-related "philanthropy" multiplies the negative economic impact hundreds of times over, leaving communities trapped in a cycle of dependency, violence, and systematic impoverishment. The facade of kindness is the tip of an iceberg of carefully calculated economic and social destruction.

AMPLIFIED TESTIMONY: ECONOMIC CANNON FODDER

Statement by Rogelio Martínez (poultry producer, Guerrero):

"We pay 'tax' even on the chickens we raise: $1 USD per bird per month. My farm has 5,000 chickens... that's $5,000 USD/month. When I protested, they burned 8,000 birds ($16,000 USD in losses). Now I'm a slave: I work 18 hours /day to pay them... and I still owe $80,000 USD for 'retroactive protection.'"

Economic impact on the chain:

1. **Perverse chaining:**
    - **Farm chicken price: $2 USD → Price with "drug tax": $3.20 USD (+60%)**
2. **Inflationary effect:**
    - **Roasted Chicken: From $6 USD to $9.50 USD (+58%)**
3. **Community consequence:**

- 72% less animal protein consumption in poor families
- 38% of children are chronically malnourished in areas controlled by the CJNG.

BRUTAL CONTRAST: THE THEATRE OF GENEROSITY

Media operation in Guerrero (Insight) Crime):

In Guerrero, the cartels' so-called "act of generosity" is more of a media spectacle than a humanitarian effort. According to Insight Crime :

• **Donation of 1,000 food parcels:** investment of $5,000 USD; however, during that same month, the cartel extorted $2 million USD from local merchants and producers.

• Photo with smiling children: coverage in three local media outlets; at the same time, 42 murders were reported that week in the area.

• **Public statement "we help the people":** represented only 0.0025% of the cartel's profits, while they maintained control over 92% of the informal economy.

Real cost-benefit analysis:

• Time to generate $2 million USD in extortion: 9.2 hours.
• Time to distribute the food supplies: 4 hours.
• Media return: 12 positive notes on local networks and media.
• Real economic return: 400 times the initial investment in "charity".

Conclusion: What appears to be community aid is, in reality, a strategic investment in legitimization and territorial control. Each "charitable" act is mere theater that conceals a flow of massive profits, violence, and systematic coercion, where the image of generosity masks a devastating economic and social impact.

MACROECONOMIC CONSEQUENCES: THE PLANNED COLLAPSE

Indicators in municipalities under drug control (CONEVAL/ CEPAL):

In municipalities under drug control, economic indicators show extreme deterioration, according to CONEVAL and ECLAC:

• **GDP per capita:** $8,500 USD in drug-free zones vs. $1,900 USD in drug-controlled zones , a 78% decrease.

• **Foreign investment:** $120 million USD/year in free zones versus $0 USD in controlled territories, a total loss of 100%.

• **Formal employment:** 68% in free zones vs. 9% under drug control, a drop of 87%.

• **Food poverty:** 18% in drug-free zones versus 94% in drug-trafficking zones, an increase of 422%.

• **Life expectancy:** 76 years in free zones compared to 58 years in drug-controlled territories, a loss of 18 years.

Documented domino effect:

Year 1:

• 40% of businesses close.
• 25% of young people migrate in search of opportunities.

Year 3:

• 90% of agricultural land abandoned. • Schools converted into drug trade logistics centers.

Year 5:

• Completely criminalized economy.
• Tortilla price increases by 300%.

DIAGRAM: THE MACHINERY OF LOOTING

[SYMBOLIC INVESTMENT]

¢¢¢ Social works (0.1% of cartel profits) | ▼ [TERRITORIAL CONTROL] ✔ ✔ ✔ Systematic extortion and economic dominance

| ▼ [COMMUNITY DESTRUCTION] ☠ Estimated damage: $18,000 USD/ha/year

| ▼ [IMAGE WASHING] Photos with food supplies, community parties → Recruitment and media legitimization

---

CONCLUSION OF THE ECONOMY OF COMMUNITY DESTRUCTION

THE CARTEL COMBINES minimal investment in "charity" with absolute economic control, creating a cycle of plunder where every "donated" dollar results in disproportionate social and economic losses. While appearing generous to the community, the drug cartel maximizes profits and systematically destroys the productive and social fabric.

At this point, it becomes clear that what we call the "narco tax" is not simply an additional cost to everyday life: it is the core of an economic system of dispossession that reshapes, step by step, the destiny of entire communities. What begins as a "discrete" fee to a merchant or producer soon becomes a network of systematic extortion that permeates every corner of social life. The result is a vicious cycle in which money flows upward—to the criminal elite—while at the bottom, only hunger, fear, and silence remain.

The contrast is stark: while families in free zones spend less than a third of their income on food, in regions controlled by cartels, that percentage can exceed 60%. This means that millions of people live in a permanent state of malnutrition, not because of drought or international crises, but because an armed group decided to turn tortillas, eggs, or liter of milk into instruments of subjugation. Violence translates into inflation, and inflation translates into hunger.

The cartels' supposed "social projects"—soccer fields, patron saint festivals, food distributions—are not altruistic gestures, but criminal marketing strategies. For every dollar invested in these handouts, thousands of dollars are extracted through extortion. The arithmetic is simple but lethal: drug traffickers invest in symbols, but they enrich themselves with lives. Every photo of smiling children hides a murder statistic; every food distribution equals dozens of ruined businesses. What we see is a carefully staged show designed to clean up an image that, at its core, thrives on bloodshed.

The community destruction they cause is not accidental: it is planned. In year one, businesses close; in year three, the land is abandoned; in year five, the legal economy has completely disappeared. A "parallel state" then emerges where the cartel controls not only violence, but also prices, mobility, and even justice. What is installed in its place is not an alternative form of government, but a criminal feudalism in which every inhabitant becomes a subject of a power that exacts tribute and punishes disobedience with death.

Beyond the numbers, the human impact is impossible to ignore. Every business that closes is a family that migrates. Every unpaid extortion is a murder. Every abandoned school is a lost generation. The real cost of drug trade is not the billions of dollars it generates, but the millions of dreams it destroys. The legacy of these communities is not wealth, but trauma: children who grow up normalizing violence, young people who see extortion as the only possible economy, adults who lose all hope of rebuilding.

But perhaps the most disturbing thing is that this model doesn't survive in isolation. The economy of community destruction is possible because there is a global system that sustains it. The dollars extorted from a farmer in Guerrero end up in banks in Switzerland or luxury towers in Miami. The chain is clear: the hunger of a child in Michoacán is the profitability of a financial broker on Wall Street. The machinery works because the gears of the local and global are perfectly synchronized.

The chapter leaves us, then, with an unavoidable conclusion: drug trade is not just an armed threat; it's a political economy of terror. Its true power lies not only in its weapons, but in its ability to control prices, inflate costs, and redraw the productive map of entire regions. Wherever it establishes itself, the community slowly dies, first economically, then socially, and finally humanly.

What remains is the most difficult question: if drug trade has succeeded in replacing the state in its basic functions—security, justice, infrastructure, and even social assistance—what alternative model can rebuild these communities? History shows that neither prohibition nor militarization has done anything but deepen the wound. The challenge is to think of a different path, one that defunds the criminal machinery and returns control of their own future to the people.

Because, in the end, what's at stake isn't just the price of a tortilla or the stability of a local business: it's the very possibility of living in community without fear. And if drug trade has proven it can destroy that possibility in five years, society must demonstrate it can rebuild it in less time. The battle, ultimately, is not against drugs or guns: it's against the economy of fear that threatens to turn an entire country into a slave territory.

Irrefutable conclusion: "The cartels execute the most efficient extractive model in history: for every dollar invested in philanthropic facades, they extract $2,500 from vulnerable communities and generate $18,000 in social damage. Their 'food pantries' are propaganda ammunition: while they give away $5 worth of food, they steal $2 million in peasant sweat. This isn't charity: it's the financial engineering of plunder that turns hunger into profit and smiles into moral alibis."

PART IV: SYSTEMIC CONNECTIONS: CORRUPTION AND WEAPONS

In December 2006, when then-President Felipe Calderón declared the formal start of the "war on drugs" in Mexico, he did so surrounded by soldiers and armor, convinced that the display of military force would be enough to recapture territories dominated by the cartels. Almost two decades later, the toll is devastating: more than 300,000 dead, 100,000 missing, hundreds of thousands displaced, and a torn social fabric that seems beyond repair. But the most disturbing aspect is not the absolute figures, but the paradox they reveal: the greater the investment in repression, the greater the growth of the economic and territorial power of drug trade.

Failure is not exclusive to Mexico. Colombia, Honduras, El Salvador, Guatemala, and even the United States have replicated the same prohibitionist and militaristic strategy for more than half a century, with identical results: a criminal industry that today moves more than $1.7 trillion annually, with profitability rates higher than those of Apple, Microsoft, or ExxonMobil. Far from extinguishing the market, repression has strengthened it, increasing drug prices, multiplying violence, and creating a criminal elite with fortunes comparable to those of global magnates.

This chapter proposes to look beyond the official narrative of "cartels" and "bosses." Drug trafficking is not simply a collection of criminal organizations; it is a transnational economic system that operates under a logic distinct from open market capitalism. Its accumulation model is more similar to medieval feudalism and colonial slavery than to corporate competition: a handful of "lords" concentrate wealth, while the base of hitmen, mules, and peasants are disposable labor subjected to debt, fear, or coercion.

In this sense, speaking of "alternative employment" in the context of drug trade is a conceptual error. This is not an informal labor market where farmers and young people find quick income; it is a regime of extreme exploitation, where human life is worth less than a rifle and where the only way out is almost always death or prison. Every dollar invested in this economy multiplies profits for the criminal elite, but it translates into bloodshed, displacement, and devastation for communities.

At the same time, the "war" has had a corrosive effect on institutions. Instead of strengthening them, militarization and the flow of international funds have opened channels of corruption that transform police, judges, and soldiers into cogs in the criminal machinery. The distinction between state and cartel becomes blurred: one provides legal cover and access to weapons, the other generates exorbitant profits. In practice, it is a hybrid joint venture , a joint business where the only losers are the citizens, who pay with taxes and lives.

The central question guiding this analysis is, then: how do we dismantle a criminal system that isn't broken, but rather functions exactly as designed, maximizing profits at the expense of human life? The answer cannot be more repression or more bullets, as half a century of evidence demonstrates their futility. The challenge is to build a new paradigm of security and development, one that directly targets the true Achilles heel of drug trade: its need to launder money and its dependence on the economic vulnerability of marginalized communities.

The following sections will first analyze the structural errors of the prohibitionist and militarized strategy, which not only failed to resolve the problem but actually exacerbated it; second, the feudal and slave-like logic underlying the drug economy, where fear becomes legal tender and the population becomes servitude; and finally, a proposal for economic denarcotization based on financial intelligence, regulation, social justice, and productive development will be outlined.

Because, in the end, drug trade is not a mythological monster alien to our societies: it is the most brutal reflection of a global system that prioritizes profit over life. And what's at stake is not just the control of territories or routes, but the very future of our communities and the possibility of building an economic order that doesn't feed on blood.

4.1 CRIMINAL SYMBIOSIS: THE WEAPONS-DRUGS MARRIAGE

THE OPERATION OF MODERN drug trade is not a unilateral activity; it is the core of a symbiotic transnational criminal ecosystem, where drug trade and arms trafficking feed each other in a feedback loop that generates power, terror, and astronomical profits. This "marriage" is not a casual alliance, but a strategic integration where each commodity strengthens the value of the other, creating a self-sustaining machine of violence whose ultimate currency is territorial control and human life.

The Symbiosis Mechanism: A Lethal Commodity Exchange

The relationship is simple in its design and brutal in its execution:

1. **Weapons provide power:** Assault rifles, ammunition, and grenades are needed to conquer cities, protect roads,

intimidate the population, and dispute territory with rivals and the state.

2. **Drugs provide capital:** Cocaine, methamphetamine, and heroin generate the cash flow needed to buy more weapons, pay hitmen, and corrupt institutions.
3. **The cycle feeds back:** More power (weapons) allows for control of more drug routes and markets, which generates more capital, which in turn finances the purchase of more and better weapons. It's an upward spiral of violence and profit.

The Map of Transnational Flows: The Geopolitics of Chaos

Data from the ATF (Alcohol, Tobacco , Firearms and Explosives) and Interpol (2024) map this global network, revealing how each continent fuels a part of the crisis:

Northern Route (USA -> Mexico): The Supermarket of Crime

- **Volume:** An estimated 210,000+ guns cross the porous U.S. southern border annually from gun shows and straw purchases. purchase " (where someone with a license buys for a third party), its destination is the Mexican cartels.

- **Cost/Benefit:** An AR-15 rifle purchased for $600 USD in Texas is resold to the cartel for $2,000-$5,000 USD. For the cartel, this is a tiny investment.
- **Humanitarian Impact:** This flow fuels a crisis of violence that contributes to the more than 34,000 organized crime-related homicides in Mexico each year. The "return" for arms traffickers is economic; for Mexican society, it is a blood bill.

Eastern Route (Europe -> Colombia): The High Technology of War

- **Volume/Method:** Military-grade weaponry (sniper rifles, grenade launchers, high-caliber assault rifles) traveling hidden in shipping containers bound for Venezuelan or Colombian ports, often acquired from diverted military stockpiles or the black market from former Balkan conflicts.
- **Cost/Benefit:** A single one of these weapons can cost $52,000 USD. Their value is not only tactical, but symbolic: they provide a brutal technological advantage over rival groups and poorly equipped police forces.
- **Humanitarian Impact:** This arms race is a direct driver of forced displacement, contributing to the number of displaced people in Colombia fleeing massacres and fighting between armed groups each year.

Western Route (Asia -> Honduras): The Weaponry of Social Control

- **Volume/Method:** Tens of thousands of semi-automatic pistols and submachine guns manufactured in China or Southeast Asia, arriving at Honduran Pacific ports to arm local cartel cells.
- **Cost/Benefit:** A weapon purchased for $18,000 USD isn't for open warfare, but for everyday territorial control: extortion, targeted killings , and intimidation. It's the tool for dominating more than 500 communities.
- **Humanitarian Impact:** Turns neighborhoods into occupied territories, where the population lives under the law of the gun.

The Lethal Equation: The Sinaloa Case - ROI of Violence

The case of the Sinaloa Cartel exemplifies the perverse financial logic of this symbiosis:

- **Initial Investment (Cost of Weapon):** $600 USD for an AR-15 rifle in the US.

- **Function 1:** Asset Protection: This rifle guards a shipment of 500 kg of cocaine.

- **Protected Asset Value:** $15,000,000 USD in the wholesale market.

- Recruitment/Control Tool: That same rifle intimidates and allows for the coercive recruitment of 48 minors for drug dealing and falconry.

Income from Labor Exploitation: These children generate approximately $14,400 USD/month in street sales.

Analyst's Conclusion: As a New York anti-drug prosecutor (2023) summarizes: "Cartels buy weapons like supermarkets: fifty rifles cost less than a kilo of cocaine in Chicago. It's the perfect business: each weapon generates profits 287 times its initial value."

Strategic Conclusion: The Architecture of Impunity

This symbiosis is not a spontaneous phenomenon; it is the operational architecture of 21st-century organized crime. It demonstrates that:

Violence is an investment tool: It's not an expense; it's the seed money for a much larger business. The profit from arms trafficking is insignificant compared to the profit enabled by the power those weapons buy.

The problem is transnational by design: No country can solve it alone. The source of the weapons, the trafficking route, the territory of impact, and the money laundering centers are often in different jurisdictions, exploiting the gaps in international cooperation.

It Feeds on Legal Asymmetries: The relative ease of acquiring weapons in one country (such as the US) becomes the greatest threat to the national security of its neighbors, creating a negative externality of catastrophic dimensions.

The fight against drug trade is, therefore, intrinsically linked to the control of illicit arms trafficking. Attacking one without the other is doomed to failure. As long as this virtuous cycle for crime (and vicious for society) remains intact, the machine of violence will continue to operate.

4.2 Structural Corruption: Officials as Shareholders

HIERARCHY OF CO-OPTATION (Transparency International):

The cartels' spectacular violence—the executions, the blockades, the narco-messages —is merely the facade of their power. Their true strength lies in a deeply rooted infrastructure of corruption that transforms the state from a contender into an accomplice. This is not a phenomenon of individual officials going rogue; it is a system of systemic co-optation where public institutions are turned into tools of illicit business. The cartels don't just bribe; they invest. And officials don't just become corrupt; they become silent shareholders in a criminal holding company, receiving dividends in exchange for armor, information, and money laundering opportunities.

The Pyramid of Co-optation: The Illegal Shareholding Structure

Transparency International 's analytical models and intelligence reports, the corruption hierarchy functions as a perverse value chain, where each level pays for a specific service and receives a criminal return on investment (ROI).

1. The Operational Base: Local and Municipal Police (Cost: ~$15,000 USD/officer/year)

- **Function:** They are the "town managers" of the status quo. Their role is not to combat crime, but to regulate it. They act as the first line of impunity.
- **Return for the Cartel:** They guarantee 92% operational impunity. They ignore crimes, warn about operations unauthorized by corrupt leaders, and allow the free movement of people and illicit goods. They are the lubricant that prevents the criminal machinery from becoming jammed.

2. The Tactical Level: Public Prosecutors and Attorneys (Cost: ~$500,000 USD/prosecutor/year)

- **Function:** They are the cartel's "corporate lawyers." Their job is to defuse any legal threats that have made it past the initial police barrier.
- **Return for the Cartel:** They manage to archive up to 78% of inconvenient cases through procedural errors, loss of evidence, witness intimidation, or simple bureaucratic inaction. They turn operational victories for federal forces into certain judicial defeats.

3. The Strategic Level: Senior Military and Federal Police Commands (Cost: ~$2 million USD/general/year)

- **Function:** They act as the internal "Board of Directors." They make decisions that affect national security in favor of the cartel.
- **Return on Investment for the Cartel:** They provide real-time intelligence: patrol routes and schedules, identities of undercover agents, operational plans. This allows the cartel to

avoid confrontations, set up selective ambushes, or eliminate specific targets. This is the level that transforms classified information into the ultimate competitive advantage.

4. The Dome: Governors, Legislators and Senior Officials (Cost: ~$10 million USD/position/year)

- **Function:** They are the " CEOs " of the symbiosis. Their work is no longer operational, but rather financial and political engineering. They create the legal and economic framework that allows crime to flourish.
- **Return for the Cartel:**

- **Macro-Scale Money Laundering**: They award inflated public contracts (infrastructure projects, health services, social programs) to cartel shell companies. The dirty money enters the public coffers as payment for a service never rendered and comes out "clean" as profit for the construction company.

- **Tailor-made legislation:** They promote or hinder laws that affect organized crime (asset forfeiture law, financial regulation, criminal proceedings).
- **Control of the Judiciary:** They appoint and place judges and magistrates who are sympathetic to them.

Expanded Emblematic Case: The Odebrecht+ Metastasis (2016-2023)

The Odebrecht scandal was just the tip of the iceberg of a much deeper and adaptive mechanism.

- **Amount Laundered:** $800 million USD (conservative estimate for Mexico and Central America only).
- **Highly Corrupt Engineering Mechanism:** This was not

limited to bribes in envelopes. A system of "ghost consultancies" and "performance bonuses" was implemented, paid through tax havens to a network of 93 high-level judges, anti-corruption prosecutors , and legislative committee presidents. These payments were tied to specific performance metrics: filing key cases, issuing predefined injunctions, and delaying vital processes.

- **Catastrophic Strategic Effect:** For seven years, this system guaranteed absolute impunity for the criminal elite. Zero key extraditions, zero convictions of kingpins, and the systematic dismantling of the most effective financial intelligence units. The state wasn't infiltrated; it was subcontracted.

Conclusion: The Privatization of Sovereignty

Structural corruption is not a "cost of doing business" for cartels; it's their most crucial investment. It allows a criminal organization to operate not from the shadows of the state, but from its offices.

The State becomes a criminal franchise: The cartel provides the business model (extortion, trafficking) and the violence; corrupt officials provide the brand, logistics, and protection. In return, they receive a commission.

The Border Is Erased: The distinction between "State" and "cartel" becomes irrelevant. The same patrols that should protect the population protect cargo; the same judges who should dispense justice acquit the kingpins; the same rulers who should develop the region launder their money.

The Strategic Defeat: Combating this reality with military operations alone is insufficient. We are fighting against an army whose headquarters are within the very institutions designed to defend society. The decisive battle is not in the streets, but in government offices, courts, and legislatures. Corruption is the most sophisticated weapon of organized crime, and until it is dismantled, violence will only be a symptom of a much deeper disease.

4.3 Money Laundering: Blood Laundering

DRUG MONEY IS A TOXIC liability. Its concentrated existence in cash is its greatest vulnerability. Therefore, the cartels have developed a global financial circulatory system comparable in sophistication to that of an investment bank, whose sole purpose is to transform blood-stained capital into legitimate, taxable, and profitable wealth. This money laundering process is not an ancillary function; it is the cornerstone that sustains the entire criminal enterprise. Without it, the business would collapse under the weight of its own illegible cash.

Documented Circuits: The Financial Engineering of Impunity

Organizations such as the FATF (Financial Action Task Force)

International) and Europol have mapped this multi-headed hydra, revealing an architecture obscene in scale and brazenness.

1. Real Estate Bribery: Miami's Luxury Vaults

- **Volume:** Approximately $12 billion annually is laundered through the purchase of ultra-luxury properties in Florida, primarily with LLCs (Limited Liability Opaque companies that hide the final beneficiary.
- **Mechanism:** People don't buy to live or rent; they buy to park capital. Apartment towers become "vertical safe deposit boxes." The property's value appreciates over time, and it can then be sold, generating a capital gain that appears legitimate. The real estate market is distorted, becoming inaccessible to local residents, while glass and steel monuments to impunity are erected.

2. Cryptocurrencies and NFTs : Digitized Opacity

- **Volume:** About $9.5 billion annually moves through this ecosystem.
- **Mechanism:** Far from limiting themselves to Bitcoin on the dark web, cartels are using " mixers " or " tumblers " (services that mix cryptocurrencies to make them irreversible), decentralized exchanges (DEXs), and the acquisition of overpriced NFTs . A "blue pixel" NFT selling for $1 million isn't an investment in art; it's a receipted, encrypted transfer of value. The buyer (the cartel) then "sells" the NFT back to themselves through an intermediary, creating a public record of a transaction that justifies the origin of illicit funds.

3. Legal Companies as a Facade: The Productive Fiction

- **Volume:** The largest channel, with an estimated $28 billion annually.
- **Mechanism:** Networks of seemingly legitimate companies—advertising agencies, construction companies, food distributors, sports clubs—are created, which fictitiously inflate their revenues. One shell company "contracts" the services of another shell company from the same cartel for an exorbitant sum. The issued invoice serves as proof of the cash deposited in the bank. The dirty money comes in as payment for a service that was never provided and comes out "clean" as business income, ready to be spent or reinvested.

4. Agricultural Commodities : The "Green Gold" of Crime

- **Volume:** Approximately $15 billion dollars annually are laundered through the export of avocados, lemons, berries , and other high-demand products.
- **Mechanism:** A cartel that controls a producing territory by force artificially inflates export volumes. It claims to ship 100

tons of avocado when it only shipped 70. The remaining 30 tons are phantom inventory whose international market value is actually drug money now appearing as legitimate profit from agricultural exports. Each box of fruit contains a hidden percentage of laundering.

The Cost of Legitimacy: The Impunity Commissions

The efficiency of this system is terrifying. The "laundering cost"—the commissions paid to complicit banks (voluntary or negligent), lawyers, notaries, financial consultants, and corrupt officials—is negligible. For every $1 of illegal money that needs to be integrated into the formal economy, the system charges a mere $0.28 in transaction fees. This is the price of erasing a blood trail: less than the cost of a beer at a luxury bar.

The Obscene Contrast: The Conversion of Life into Luxury

This machinery allows for contrasts that encapsulate the entire perversion of the system:

- Patek Philippe watch ($250,000 USD) = The combined lifetime salary of 17 hitmen (calculated on a 5-year criminal work life expectancy at $300/month).
- 1 private party in Ibiza for the son of a drug lord ($600,000 USD) = The value of the blood of 420 falcon children (calculated on a monthly "payroll" of $120 per child for one year of exploitation). Human life is the cheapest commodity in this equation.

Conclusion: The Final Phase of the Crime

Money laundering is the final stage of criminal alienation. It completely disconnects the violent act (murder, kidnapping, drug dealing) from the ultimate profit (the yacht, the penthouse, the work of art). It allows the bosses not only to enjoy the loot, but to do so in full view, like respectable magnates, philanthropists, and patrons.

It's a globalized industry based in tax havens, Wall Street law firms, and Dubai real estate developments. Its existence demonstrates that the global financial system has weak antibodies against poisonous capital when it arrives in sufficiently large volumes and accompanied by generous commissions.

Therefore, combating drug trade without strangling its financial flows is a losing battle. As long as mechanisms exist to launder blood, there will always be incentives to shed it. Money laundering is not a complementary crime; it is the very heart of the modern criminal enterprise.

4.4 Parallel Economies: Ghost States

CRIMINAL SUBSTITUTION indicators (IDB 2024):

The most advanced and dangerous phenomenon of organized crime is not its ability to challenge the state, but to replace it. In vast areas of Latin America, cartels have evolved from mere criminal organizations to parallel governance entities, building "ghost states" that compete with—and surpass—the legitimate state in the provision of essential services, but with a diametrically opposed objective: not the common good, but the maximization of criminal control. The Inter-American Development Bank (2024) documents this substitution not as a one-off failure, but as an alternative and functional system of power whose indicators reveal a perverse logic of predatory efficiency.

The Pillars of the Phantom State: A Perverse Offer of "Governance"

The substitution occurs in all areas that traditionally define a state's sovereignty, creating a distorted and brutal mirror of public administration.

1. The Monopoly of Violence: Security as Control

- **The Legitimate State:** It operates with a ratio of 1 police officer for every 500 inhabitants, a symbolic, reactive, and completely insufficient figure dedicated to the prosecution of minor crimes.
- **The Criminal State:** It deploys an occupation force with a ratio of one hitman or hawk for every 20 inhabitants. This is not a security force, but rather one of total social control. Its function is not to prevent crime, but to enforce the cartel's law, ensuring criminal order, deterring competition, and monitoring the population. It is an omnipresent and intimidating presence.

2. The Administration of Justice: The "Fugitive Law" vs. Bureaucracy

- **The Legitimate State:** Its courts operate with a 12% efficiency rate (case resolution rates). Justice is slow, corruptible, and perceived as inaccessible.
- **The Criminal State:** It offers expeditious "justice" based on the principle of "ley fuga" or summary trial. Its effectiveness is 100%: the sentence (usually death or mutilation) is carried out immediately and without appeal. It is a brutal system, but for a desperate population, it can seem more effective than state impunity. It resolves property disputes, personal vendettas, and business disputes under its own rules.

3. Infrastructure and Logistics: Building for Illicit Trade

- **The Legitimate State:** Builds an average of 0.7 km of rural roads per year, a victim of bureaucracy, corruption, and underdevelopment.

- **The Criminal State:** Develops 15 km of "narco-roads" in the same period. This infrastructure is not for community development; it is a capital investment in criminal logistics. It improves the efficiency of drug, arms, and human trafficking, reduces operating costs, and consolidates territorial control. It is a demonstration of power and effectiveness that the State cannot match.

4. Social Assistance and Economy: The Narco- Welfare State

- **The Legitimate State:** Distributes symbolic aid of approximately $120 USD per family per year.
- **The Criminal State:** It implements a system of "handouts" or "narco-assistance" that provides $40 USD per family per month ($480 USD/year). This apparent generosity is actually a cycle of dependency financed by the very violence that sustains it: the money distributed comes from extortion paid by the community itself. It is a scheme of image laundering and control that creates a perverse obligation and deactivates resistance.

Case Study: Guerrero, Mexico (Proceso, 2023) - Health as an Operational Investment

The Guerrero case exemplifies how substitution is strategic and focuses on areas critical to the cartel's operations.

- **The Legitimate State:** Allocated $1.2 million to rural clinics, which often lack medicines, equipment, and staff, symbolizing abandonment.
- **The Criminal State:** Invested $8.5 million in high-performance clandestine clinics. These facilities are not designed for the general population; they are the equivalent of corporate medical services for its workforce. Their purpose is

clear:

- Treat gunshot wounds immediately and discreetly, preventing hitmen from reaching public hospitals where they would be arrested.
- Perform reconstructive surgeries on bosses.
- Maintain the productivity and morale of your "army."

This investment isn't charity; it's the maintenance of armed human capital. It ensures that their most valuable asset (violent force) remains operational.

Conclusion: The Competition for Legitimacy and the Efficiency of Terror

The result of this comprehensive substitution is the emergence of functioning "ghost states." The population trapped in these territories no longer judges based on the legitimacy of origin (elected government vs. criminal organization), but rather on perceived effectiveness.

- **The Cartel offers:** immediate (albeit brutal) order, rapid conflict resolution, (illegal) employment, and a constant presence.
- **The State offers:** Abandonment, bureaucracy, impunity and a sporadic and often corrupt presence.

This perverse competition creates a "legitimacy by default" for the cartel. It is not won by consensus, but because it is the only entity that appears and makes decisions. The Phantom State does not seek development; it seeks the stability necessary to optimize its illicit businesses. This is the ultimate form of territorial capture: it no longer infiltrates the State, but builds a new one in its image, where the currency is not taxes, but submission and life itself. The reconquest of these territories requires not only security operations, but a genuine, constant, and more powerful State offering than the perverse efficiency of crime.

SUMMARY TABLE: THE IMPUNITY RACE

The race for impunity

The criminal structure is sustained not only by direct violence, but also by a set of economic and political mechanisms that reinforce its permanence. Each cog in this machine has a clear reversal, a devastating social cost, and a historical echo.

Arms trafficking represents an investment of approximately $150 million annually, resulting in a tragic toll: one death every minute in Mexico. This dynamic is reminiscent of the brutality of the 18th-century slave trade, where the trade in human bodies sustained the economies of entire empires.

Corruption acts as a lubricant for the system. Cartels spend an average of $2.8 million a day to guarantee their institutional protection, generating a 94% level of impunity. In historical memory, this phenomenon evokes the banana republic dictatorships, where institutions were mere extensions of mafia or corporate power.

Money laundering operates with an almost mathematical logic: 28 cents for every dirty dollar is enough to give it the appearance of legality. Behind this facade lie at least 800 active tax havens, a global money laundering scheme comparable to extractive colonialism, where the wealth of a continent was siphoned off into protected enclaves.

Finally, the consolidation of the parallel state reflects the magnitude of criminal domination. These structures now represent nearly 15% of the regional GDP, with a direct impact on 42 million people living under drug control. The model resembles criminal feudalism, where the entire community is subject to the protection and violence of a warlord.

Taken together, these mechanisms are not anomalies, but rather a systematic race for impunity, combining financial resources, organized violence, and structural complicity to reshape entire territories.

ANALYSIS: THE GLOBAL CARTEL

"This isn't a criminal network: it's a transnational conglomerate based on impunity. Its CEOs are drug lords who buy senators cheaper than rifles; its shareholders are banks that launder blood at $0.28 per dollar; its end consumers are societies addicted to forgetting. While a child hitman dies for $0.13 a bullet, a banker in Zurich earns $2,800 laundering that same death. Drug trafficking isn't a security issue: it's predatory capitalism in its final phase."

—Carlo Bonini , organized crime investigator

Organized crime can no longer be understood as a marginal phenomenon, isolated on the periphery. Today, it operates as a global cartel, a corporate holding company governed by the same logic as any multinational corporation: profit maximization, cost reduction, and market expansion. The difference is that its raw material is human life, and its competitive advantage is impunity.

Each gear confirms the business architecture of drug trade:

- Weapons flow from the U.S. to Latin America at a rate of more than 210,000 pieces per year, fueling a cycle of violence that leaves one death every minute in Mexico.
- Financial laundering turns billions into clean capital. With just $0.28 for every dirty dollar, global banks ensure the blood disappears from their balance sheets.
- Bribes are distributed as political dividends: from $15,000 per local police officer to $10 million per governor, buying silence and shielding.
- Parallel states are consolidating their dominance: they now represent 15% of the regional GDP and subject more than 42

million people to feudal territorial control.

The criminal map is also a corporate map:

- Red arrows indicate the flow of weapons from Texas to the entire continent.
- Black arrows follow the reverse path of dirty money toward Europe and Asia.
- Green arrows reveal the constant flow of bribes to key officials.
- Shaded areas mark territories where drug trade has already replaced the State.

The so-called "war on drugs" fails because it attacks the symptoms, not the system. It attacks the rank-and-file soldiers but leaves the four pillars that support the criminal edifice intact: arms trafficking, structural corruption, money laundering, and the creation of parallel economies.

The result is a paradox: while peasants, migrants, and young people are being killed in the periphery, in the financial centers of the North, crime is being transformed into bonuses, dividends, and surplus value. The global cartel is, in reality, an obscene version of financial capitalism, a mirror in which corporate power and organized violence are now indistinguishable.

Final conclusion: *There is no cartel without a bank, no hitman without an imported rifle, no impunity without a bought-off official. What we call "organized crime" is not the exception: it's the rule of the system.*

SYSTEMIC LINKS (Focus: Financial Flows)

Economic analysis of the corruption-arms-money laundering symbiosis

1. CORRUPTION DIAGRAMS: THE IMPUNITY MARKET

Corruption is not a byproduct of drug trade: it is its accounting engine. If the drug business were a transnational corporation, bribes would be its public relations budget, its investment in political marketing to ensure operational stability. Data from Transparency International (2024) show that cartels allocate between 10% and 30% of their total profits to direct bribe payments, equivalent to a global flow of nearly $18 billion per year.

These payments are neither improvised nor random. They operate under a hierarchy of tiered co-optation, where each level of the state apparatus has a price and a profit margin:

- **Local police:** They receive between $15,000 and $50,000 annually for their silence or complicity. They represent about 30% of bribe spending, as they are the first line of defense that can stop a shipment or release a detainee.
- **Prosecutors:** With amounts ranging from $200,000 to $500,000 annually, they ensure that files are not misplaced, evidence is "lost," and investigations are quietly closed. Their share of the chain accounts for 25% of the spending.
- **Judges:** More expensive but decisive, with fees ranging from $500,000 to $1 million a year, they absorb 20% of bribes. With a single signature, they can acquit a drug lord or overturn a historic conviction.
- **Senior executive officials:** governors, ministers, or heads of national security, whose pay is around $5 to $10 million a year. They represent 15% of spending, but their cover is strategic: they shield entire public policies.
- **High-level politicians:** senators, representatives, and party leaders. Here, the fee starts at $10 million annually, with a 10% cut of the spending in bribes. Their power lies in tailoring legislation, blocking uncomfortable reforms, or facilitating multimillion-dollar concessions.

The result is a system where impunity ceases to be a flaw and becomes a market commodity, a profitable service acquired by the cartels as naturally as a shipment of weapons.

Colombia case: anatomy of political buying

The Colombian experience documented by the Electoral Observation Mission (MOE, 2023) starkly illustrates the scope of this phenomenon. In that country, 63% of municipalities have proven links between criminal structures and local political authorities. The mechanism is simple: of each municipal budget, an average of 22% is allocated to bribes and illicit deals.

The payback is devastating: the cartels enjoy 98% impunity in their operations, a margin of safety that exceeds any investment in logistics or weapons. In other words, in Colombia—and replicated throughout much of Latin America—corruption is not a secondary expense, but rather the cheapest and most effective insurance policy for organized crime.

Structural connection

When analyzing the corruption-arms-laundering triangle, corruption appears as the invisible glue that connects the other two axes. Without co-opted judges and politicians, rifle shipments would be intercepted and dirty dollars would be stranded in cash. Corruption, in its systematic and hierarchical form, ensures that the circuit flows uninterrupted.

What emerges is not a "weak state," as is often claimed, but a commodified state, where legality has a price and institutional loyalty is auctioned off to the highest bidder.

---

2. COST-EFFICIENCY OF ARMS TRAFFICKING: THE LETHAL EQUATION

AR-47 Analysis (Source: ATF, Europol 2024):

The AR-47 rifle has become the most efficient accounting instrument of drug trade. It's not just a weapon: it's an investment with the highest return for organized crime. According to data from the ATF and Europol (2024), the average acquisition cost of a rifle in the U.S. market is around $300, plus clandestine transportation to Mexico at $150 per piece. In other words, for $450, a cartel can arm a hitman with the necessary tools to maintain its territorial dominance.

The lethal factor lies in the following mathematics. That cheap rifle, which costs less than a high-end phone, becomes a criminal profit-making machine:

- He can sustain 500 extortion acts, at a rate of $50 per victim, generating about $25,000.
- It serves as collateral for 200 "rented" homicides, each valued at $500, representing an additional $100,000.
- But the greatest benefit comes from controlling the territory. A rifle can hold a strategic area under control for at least six months, which translates into an income of $375,000 from drug exploitation, protection rackets, kidnappings, and trafficking.

The initial investment of $450 turns into half a million dollars in profit, equivalent to a return on investment (ROI) of 1.111 to 1. No legitimate financial product on Wall Street can compete with that equation.

An anti-drug prosecutor interviewed by the New York Times (2023) summed it up bluntly:

"A rifle costs less than an iPhone, but generates more profit than an apartment in Miami."

The weapon as a "financial asset"

In the drug-related ecosystem, the rifle is not seen as a military expense, but as a liquid financial asset. Unlike drugs, which are consumed and then disappear, or cash, which requires laundering, the rifle retains its value and multiplies its usefulness. A single rifle can be used to intimidate dealers, assassinate rivals, keep entire communities under control, and secure cocaine shipments.

The equation is brutally efficient: $450 → $500,000, multiplied by tens of thousands of rifles per year. In practice, the cartels have turned arms trafficking into the most profitable product of criminal capitalism.

Historical comparison

The cost-benefit ratio of the AR-47 rifle is reminiscent of other moments in history where cheap items generated immense fortunes. In the 18th century, for example, a European musket sold in Africa for a few coins became the key to capturing slaves, whose sale in the Caribbean yielded profits multiplied by a hundred. The arms trade in the 21st century repeats the same logic: cheap Western goods fuel a cycle of violence that generates extraordinary rents in the periphery.

Structural connection

This analysis demonstrates that drug trade not only traffics drugs, but also finances violence with weapons subsidized by the U.S. market. While Congress debates minimum sales restrictions, the cartels have found the most reliable branch of their war economy in the gun shops of South Texas.

In strictly economic terms, each rifle is an investment with a better return than oil, gold, or Bitcoin. And while financial statistics confirm this, the social statistics are even more relentless: each rifle smuggled into Mexico translates into one life lost every minute, in a war that enriches a few and devours millions.

---

3. INTERNATIONAL WASHING: THE PERFECT WHITENING

Shocking facts (UNODC, FATF 2024):

Drug money laundering is not a simple financial trick: it is a perfectly calibrated global system that turns blood and fear into legitimate goods. According to UNODC and the FATF (2024), barely

0.2% of laundered money is seized each year, demonstrating the system's almost absolute impunity. Annual flows are estimated to reach $2.3 trillion, equivalent to Italy's GDP, distributed among banks, legal companies, and offshore circuits .

An emblematic example is the HSBC case (2012), where the bank facilitated the laundering of $881 million, received a $1.9 billion fine, but kept 98.7% of the illicit profits. The math is clear: financial institutions act as co-conspirators in the crime, absorbing the risk in exchange for commissions and marginal profits.

Documented international circuits (Europol)

Cartel money follows a structured path:

[Capos] → [Banks] → [Legal Sectors]

Within the legal sectors, flows are divided roughly as follows:

- 45% to luxury real estate (Miami, Dubai), with "empty" towers serving as wealth stores.
- 30% to cryptocurrencies and abstract art NFTs , intangible assets that are difficult to track.
- 15% on commodities such as avocado, lemon, gold, and oil, camouflaging illicit profits in exports.
- 10% to sports clubs and franchises, which function as a social and symbolic money laundering scheme, in addition to covert marketing.
- Obscene contrast: the value of blood
- The scale of this whitewashing is chilling:
- A $5 million apartment in Miami is equivalent, in terms of direct violence, to the blood of 2,500 hitmen.
- A $690,000 abstract art NFT represents the lifetime debt owed by 78 cartel recruits.

Every laundered dollar isn't just money; it's a life consumed, a community suffocated, a cycle of perpetual debt. The figures show that drug trade not only generates physical violence, but has also created a global system of criminal investment, where death is transformed into liquid capital, protected by international banks and sophisticated legal markets.

Simply put, international money laundering transforms horror into untouchable financial assets, and while the kingpins sit on yachts in Dubai, millions of families continue to pay the price in blood, fear, and poverty.

---

4. HISTORICAL PARALLEL: CORRUPTION AS A CONSTANT

Bribes in Potosí (1545-1825) vs. Narco Bribes (2024):

Corruption is not a new phenomenon in Latin America; it is a structural constant that has accompanied the extraction of wealth from the Viceroyalty to the era of drug trade. An emblematic example is the mines of Potosí (1545-1825), where the "Royal Fifth," a tax equivalent to 15% of production, was channeled to viceroys and foremen. This systematic extraction led to the deaths of approximately 8 million people, including indigenous people and imported slaves, leaving a legacy of exploitation and inequality.

Today, in the 21st century, cartels replicate this pattern in new forms: the "systemic kickback." Between 10 and 30% of their profits are used to bribe generals, prosecutors, and key officials, ensuring impunity in Mexico, where at least 500,000 drug-related deaths were recorded between 2006 and 2024.

The efficiency of evil

The historical parallel is not merely symbolic: drug trade has perfected the economic calculation of violence. According to recent analyses:

- **Bribes:** By investing just 15% of their profits, cartels achieve 92% impunity, equivalent to a 613% return on investment.
- **Guns:** Purchasing a $450 USD rifle can generate up to

$500,000 USD in profit, with an ROI of 111,100%.

- **Money laundering:** Every illicit dollar transformed into a clean $0.998 demonstrates 99.8% efficiency, with virtually no losses.

Integrated case: the perfect circle

Operation "White Shadows" (Sinaloa-Medellín, 2023) exemplifies the synergy of corruption, violence and money laundering:

1. **Gun Purchase in Texas:** $500,000 USD to purchase 1,000 rifles.
2. **Bribes in Colombia:** $2 million USD distributed among 12 judges to ensure legal protection.
3. **Cocaine production:** 5 tons with a street value of $150 million USD.
4. **International Laundering:** Swiss Real Estate and NFTs , Generating $147 Million in Net Cash

Final net profit: $144.5 million USD.

Human cost: 214 direct deaths, including 32 children, and 5 communities displaced.

This case demonstrates how cartels have replicated and refined historical methods of wealth extraction: combining violence, bribery, and money laundering to maximize profits while minimizing financial risks. History shows that systematic corruption is the common thread between extractive colonialism and modern drug trade, and that every dollar "invested" in impunity produces a devastating return for society.

EPILOGUE: THE IMPUNITED MACHINERY

"These financial flows reveal the true criminal globalization: rifles that travel 48 hours from Houston to Culiacán, cocaine traveling from Colombia, money laundered in Switzerland and Dubai, and accomplices in every capital of the world. An AK-47 purchased for

$450 USD can generate more profit—$500,000 USD—than an average Mexican worker earns in 82 years of working life. Meanwhile, banks launder 99.8% of this blood for practically pennies on the dollar, and officials replicate the logic of the colonial 'royal fifth,' ensuring impunity and continued plunder. This is not organized crime: it's cannibalistic capitalism, where human life is worth less than the transport of a rifle."

—Carlo Bonini, The Economics of Blood

Conceptual diagram of criminal flow

Drug trafficking is not an anomaly in the global economic system: it is its most blatant expression. The money trail reveals a circular logic in which every dollar invested is multiplied thousands of times thanks to the fusion of three mechanisms: violence (guns), prohibition (drugs), and money laundering (banks and tax havens). The system works not because the law fails, but because the law becomes the main input of the business: prohibition raises prices, corruption opens doors, and impunity guarantees continuity.

Conceptual diagram of criminal flow

Arms trafficking

Initial investment: $450 USD per rifle purchased in Texas.

This rifle isn't just a weapon: it's a financial machine. It allows for holding territories under criminal control, carrying out massive extortions, and displacing communities.

▼

Drug production and trafficking

With a rifle secured, the production of cocaine, marijuana, or methamphetamines is protected.

In the case of cocaine, 5 tons have a street value of $150 million USD in New York or London.

▼

Bribes

At least 15% of the profits (about $22.5 million USD in this example) are used to buy loyalty within the police, military, and political circles. It's the most profitable investment: for every dollar invested in bribery, the cartels get six dollars in impunity.

▼

Money laundering

Once in the banking system, dirty money is "cleaned" with 99.8% efficiency. It flows to Dubai, Miami, Panama, Zurich, and London. There, it is converted into empty luxury towers, digital artwork (NFTs), football player contracts, or exports of legal commodities like avocados and lemons.

▼

"Legal" investment

The transformed capital returns as a respectable investment: hotels, construction companies, advertising agencies. The circle closes: criminal wealth becomes institutionalized, and drug traffickers are no longer seen as criminals, but as philanthropic entrepreneurs who finance political campaigns or open schools.

Return and final calculation

The cost-benefit analysis is brutal:

- Every $1 USD invested in this circuit produces a net return of $300,000 USD clean.
- A $450 AR-15 rifle can support operations that generate more economic value than a mid-sized firm on Wall Street.
- The "human cost" is invisible in the balance sheets, but devastating: each weapon equals 10 lives lost, each shipment means thousands displaced, and each laundered dollar reproduces structural inequality.

FINAL ANALYSIS

THIS SYSTEM ISN'T BROKEN: it's designed for predation. It operates as a global machine that concentrates wealth in the hands of a criminal-financial elite, while externalizing all costs to the most vulnerable communities. Narcotics are capitalism in its purest form: a modern feudalism that combines violence, speculation, and human extractivism . The result is a historical paradox: the "war on drugs" doesn't combat narcotics, but rather legitimizes them as a central economic actor, while turning entire states into outsourced managers of a globalized criminal economy.

The historical, economic, and social evidence reviewed throughout this chapter reveals a relentless diagnosis: the so-called "war on drugs" failed not for lack of bullets or soldiers, but because it was doomed to absurdity from its very design. Instead of weakening organized crime, it fueled it with resources, made it more violent and fragmented, and eroded to the core the state institutions charged with combating it.

Drug trafficking, far from being an isolated criminal problem, operates as a parallel economic system with its own logic: it concentrates wealth in the hands of a tiny elite, exploits disposable labor under mechanisms of fear and debt, and parasitizes communities until they are left in ruins. Its structure does not resemble a modern business, but rather a feudal regime that controls lives and territories through invisible chains forged in terror.

The great structural discovery is that the true Achilles heel of drug trade is not the hitmen or the drug shipments, but its imperative need to integrate trillions of dollars of illicit proceeds into the global economy. Therein lies its vulnerability, and, paradoxically, it is there that states have been weakest: while billions are spent on helicopters and rifles, only a tiny fraction is invested in financial intelligence, asset prosecution, or transnational cooperation to dismantle money laundering networks.

At the same time, comparative case studies show that alternatives do exist. Community programs in Medellín reduced youth recruitment by almost half; the Portuguese model demonstrated that treating drug use as a public health issue, rather than a crime issue, reduces deaths and violence; and testimonies from former recruits reveal that legitimate economic competition can replace criminal wages when there is access to real, productive projects.

The conclusion is clear: the future of anti-drug policy lies not in more war, but in a strategic shift toward economic denarcotization. This involves three inseparable fronts:

1. Stifling criminal capital through financial intelligence, global sanctions, and digital asset regulation.
2. Building resilient local economies makes legal employment a more profitable option than drug trade.
3. Restore institutional legitimacy, not with rhetoric, but with practices of transparency, effective justice, and social reparation.

In other words, real victory is not won in the mountains of Sinaloa or the jungles of Putumayo, but in the accounting books, in international courts, and in the labor markets where the fate of millions of young people is contested. The war that failed was the one of bullets; the one that can still be won is the one of money, justice, and opportunity.

PART V: ANATOMY OF FAILURE: THE FAILED WAR

An economic analysis of four decades of strategic errors shows that the so-called "war on drugs" has not only failed but has strengthened the very system it sought to destroy. Few public policies in contemporary history have had such widespread consensus regarding their failure as the so-called war on drugs. Born in the 1970s under the rhetoric of protecting youth, preserving public health, and dismantling criminal groups, it soon became a sustained global crusade for more than half a century, replicated on various continents and financed with colossal resources. However, the figures reveal a devastating picture: consumption did not decrease, the cartels did not disappear, and violence multiplied.

The logic of this war was based on a simple, almost intuitive premise: if drug production and trade are prohibited, the market will disappear. In practice, the opposite occurred. Prohibition did not extinguish demand, but rather generated a criminal ecosystem where risk was translated into profit and violence into a method of competition. The result was the creation of the most profitable illicit business in the world, with revenues exceeding the GDP of many middle-income countries.

The impact is not limited to the economic sphere. The war on drugs has shaped Latin American geopolitics, militarized entire societies, and reconfigured the relationship between states and citizens.

What began as a security strategy became a laboratory of authoritarianism, corruption, and institutional erosion. From Mexico to Colombia, passing through Central America and the Caribbean, nations were trapped in a vicious cycle: each captured drug lord generated three new leaders; each military operation opened more fronts for violence; every dollar invested ended up converted into capital for organized crime.

This war, which was never a war but a business, reveals a pattern of strategic errors that are repeated with surgical precision: policies of prohibition that multiply criminal profits, militarization that professionalizes violence, institutions corroded from within, and an international system that, far from weakening the phenomenon, normalized it as a structural part of the global economy.

The following pages will explore the anatomy of this failure, not as a succession of isolated errors, but as the logical consequence of a model that was flawed from its inception. Analyzing prohibitionism, militarization, institutional corruption, and the comparative experiences of Mexico and Colombia not only allows us to understand why this war was lost from the start, but also to chart the paths out of a conflict that has left millions of victims and that, without a radical paradigm shift, will continue to spiral downward.

5.1 Prohibitionism: The Mistake That Multiplied Profits

THE "WAR ON DRUGS," based on the prohibitionist paradigm, constitutes one of the greatest public policy and geopolitical errors of the last century. Far from eradicating the phenomenon, it served as the greatest catalyst for criminal innovation and illicit capital accumulation in modern history. By criminalizing supply and pursuing demand without extinguishing it, prohibitionism did not eliminate the market; it transformed it into an ultra-profitable, violent monopoly , free of taxes, regulations, and legal competition, where the risk of prohibition translated directly into an exorbitant premium on the final price. It was an involuntary state subsidy for violence.

The Fundamental Economics of the Black Market: The Iron Law of Prohibition

The mechanism is simple and is governed by predictable economic principles:

1. **Creating Artificial Scarcity:** Prohibition does not eliminate desire (demand), but it does severely restrict supply.
2. **Exploding Profit Margins:** The risk of producing, transporting, and selling illegal goods must be offset by an astronomically higher final price. Each barrier (borders, operations) adds a "risk tax" paid by the end consumer and pocketed by the trafficker.
3. **Elimination of Peaceful Competition:** In a legal market, companies compete on price, quality, and marketing. In a black market, competition is resolved with violence. The most brutal, not the most efficient, remains a monopoly.

The Rebound Effect in Numbers: Failure Measured in Trillions (UNODC, 2024)

Figures from the United Nations Office on Drugs and Crime are irrefutable testimony to the colossal failure:

Price of Cocaine (kg in NYC):

- 1971 (Start of the War): ~$25,000 USD
- **2024: ~$150,000 USD**
- Increase: +500%

Analysis: The persecution didn't make the product cheaper; it made it obscenely more expensive. Each successful seizure, by temporarily reducing the available supply, increased the price of the remaining drugs, benefiting the cartels that managed to smuggle their merchandise.

Global Profits from Drug Trafficking:

- 1971: ~$100 billion USD
- 2024: ~$1.7 trillion USD
- Increase: +1,600%

Analysis: The "war" didn't restrict the income from crime; it multiplied it by 17. The business is now more lucrative than the oil industry in many countries.

Global Consumer Base:

- 1971: ~180 million people
- 2024: ~620 million people
- Increase: +244%

Analysis: *Prohibitionism failed in its central objective: to reduce consumption. The drug, transformed into a forbidden and mythologized fruit, saw its market expand globally.*

Historical Paradox: Lessons Not Learned from the Failed Experiment

History had already provided an instruction manual for disaster: Prohibition in the United States (1920-1933).

The Mirror of Prohibition: Designed to protect public morals, its only achievement was to create the perfect black market. Figures like Al Capone emerged overnight , building empires that generated profits equivalent to $300 billion annually in today's dollars.

The Global Repetition (1971–2024): Drug prohibition repeated the pattern, but with exponentially more lethal consequences. Alcohol mafias, confined to one city and wielding shotguns, morphed into transnational cartels. These new actors are 23 times richer than Al Capone at his peak, operate with military-grade weaponry, maintain private armies, and exert effective territorial control over parts of entire continents. Prohibition didn't learn from the past; it escalated it.

Structural Consequence: The Professionalization of Barbarism

Far from "fighting" the business, prohibitionism industrialized and professionalized it:

From Subsistence to Global Crime: It transformed the poor peasant, who grew coca or poppies to supplement his income, into an exploited link in a global extractive value chain, connecting the mountains of Guerrero or the Andes with the streets of London or Sydney.

Criminal Corporate Evolution: It transformed local gangs into vertically integrated criminal corporations. These "companies" have logistics, finance (money laundering), human resources (recruitment), security (hitmen), and public relations (drug trade and welfare) departments.

The World's Most Profitable Commodity: In the regions under their control, a kilo of cocaine or heroin has a profitability per kilo/m2 that far exceeds that of gold, oil, or lithium. It is the most valuable illegal natural resource on the planet.

Conclusion: War as a Perverse Subsidy

The end result of four decades of prohibition is a tragic paradox: every bullet fired, every trumpeted operation, every captured drug lord has ultimately been a subsidy to the economy it was intended to destroy.

The dynamic is perverse:

1. A military operation seizes 10 tons of cocaine.
2. The supply available on the global market is temporarily reduced.

3. The law of supply and demand raises the price of the remaining kilo.
4. The cartels that were not affected saw their profits multiplied by the very action that was intended to harm them.
5. Weakened cartels are absorbed by more violent and efficient ones, further centralizing criminal power.

The "war" was never a war; it was a perverse stimulus cycle that made products more expensive, strengthened the most ruthless actors, and ensured that the flow of blood and money from producing countries to the financial centers of Wall Street and London never stopped. Prohibitionism is not the solution; it is the driving force of the problem.

5.2 Counterproductive Militarization: Violence as a Business

THE "FRONTAL WAR" STRATEGY based on militarization not only failed to weaken organized crime; it acted as an unintentional catalyst that transformed it into a more violent, decentralized, and economically resilient entity. Far from being a solution, militarization became a key input into the criminal ecosystem, fueling a cycle of violence that benefited both the cartels and external actors who supplied weapons and equipment. This doctrine failed to understand that organized crime is not a conventional army, but a virus that mutates and strengthens with each frontal attack.

Balance Mexico 2006-2024 (SEDENA / CIDAC):

Official figures paint a picture of colossal effort and inverted results:

Military and Security Spending: $120 billion USD was invested in equipment, operations, and salaries. No cartel was permanently eliminated. Instead, groups recombined, splintered, and grew stronger.

The Disarmament Farce: 580,000 rifles were seized. However, during the same period, 2.1 million new guns were smuggled from the United States, primarily through the "accordion effect" (legal purchase in the U.S. and illegal trafficking to Mexico). For every gun seized, nearly four new ones entered the country.

The " Kingpin" Strategy " and its Hydra Effect: 120 high-profile criminal leaders were captured or eliminated. The consequence was not dismantling, but fragmentation and the emergence of 450 new leaders in more aggressive and less negotiable structures. Cutting off the head did not kill the hydra; it multiplied it.

Each "successful" operation opened the way for a generational change and multiplied the number of middle managers, like corporate hydras: cutting off one head meant three more would appear.

The "Balloon Effect" in Action: The RAND Corporation Case Study (2023)

A RAND Corporation study documented with surgical precision the vicious cycle unleashed by a massive operation in Michoacán:

Compression Phase (Year 1): The concentrated military operation achieved a 40% reduction in violence rates in the immediate area of action. This was marketed in the media as a "resounding success."

Realignment and Expansion Phase (Year 2): Pressure did not eliminate criminal groups; it displaced and fragmented them. Violence did not disappear; it redistributed geographically, erupting with a ferocity of +230% in neighboring states like Jalisco and Guanajuato, where groups fought over new territories and routes.

Final Fragmentation Phase (Outcome 2024): The national criminal structure fragmented. From six relatively identifiable national cartels, it evolved into 22 hyper-violent regional groups (Jalisco New Generation Cartel, Cartel del Noreste, La Familia Michoacana, etc.), which are much more difficult to map, negotiate, and combat.

Paradoxical End Result: Total drug profits increased by 300% during the decade. Militarization didn't destroy the market; it made it more efficient, more expensive, and therefore more profitable. Violence was an operating cost that, when increased, raised the final price of the product.

The Three Structural Paradoxes of Militarization

The failed strategy is based on three fundamental paradoxes that explain its counterproductivity:

1. **Militarization Fuels the Industry of Violence:**

The constant military presence doesn't deter; it professionalizes rival violence. Cartels are forced to:

- Invest in better weapons to confront the State, increasing its firepower.
- Recruit more hitmen to compensate for the losses, often recruiting in a more forced and violent manner.
- Innovate in tactics (use of drones, booby traps, homemade armor).

  This turns violence into another production input. State war doesn't eliminate business; it makes entry more expensive and consolidates the power of the strongest and most brutal actors.

1. **Militarization as a Theater of Political Legitimation:**

Governments confuse activity with results. Every spectacular capture (even if strategically irrelevant) and every media operation serve to simulate control and decisive action in the face of a demanding public opinion. Short-term communication impact is prioritized over long-term strategic effectiveness. It's a policy for the chambers, not for the communities.

1. **The Transnational War Economy: The Iron Circle:**

This is the most cynical point of all: the same system that supplies weapons to the cartel sells solutions to the State.

- The cartel buys assault weapons in Texas (90% of the weapons seized in Mexico are of US origin).
- To combat this, the Mexican state spends billions on purchasing Black Hawk helicopters, high-precision rifles, and communications equipment, also from American companies.
- Mexican and U.S. taxpayer money ends up funding both sides of the conflict, enriching the arms industry. It's a perverse economic feedback loop where violence is business and peace, its downfall.

Critical Synthesis

Militarization did not diminish the cartels' violence or economic power. On the contrary:

- **It raised the human costs:** more than 500,000 deaths and 400,000 displaced people in Mexico (2006-2024).
- **It consolidated a parallel war economy**, where both crime and the state are supplied by the same arms industry.
- **It generated a market dynamic that rewards fragmentation:** more small groups, more disputed territories, more diversified businesses (huachicol, trafficking, fentanyl).

In the words of a former DEA official: *"The war on drugs is the first war in history where every bullet fired guarantees the enemy will make more money."*

Conclusion: Defeat by Design

Militarization as a central strategy is a catastrophic misdiagnosis. It treats a symptom (violence) with a dose of the same poison (more violence), ignoring the disease: social breakdown, lack of opportunity, and the economic integration of crime.

The result is not pacification, but the normalization of war. The cartels are no longer gangs; they are belligerent enterprises capable of challenging the state. The strategy of frontal war didn't destroy them; it trained them, equipped them, and made them stronger. The only valid lesson is that you can't burn down your house to scare away the rats; you only succeed in burning down your house and breeding more fire-resistant rats. The solution requires dismantling the economic incentives for crime, not multiplying those of its war industry.

5.3 Institutional Erosion: When the Anti-Drug Force Finances the Narcotics

THE SO-CALLED "WAR on drugs" has demonstrated a boomerang effect: the same public funds intended to combat drug trade end up fattening criminal coffers. Institutional corruption is not an accident; it's the central link that turns anti-drug policy into investment capital for the cartels.

Documented cases of anti-drug corruption

Mexico (2023): The Gendarmerie at the service of the CJNG

An official report revealed that the National Gendarmerie maintained ties to the Jalisco New Generation Cartel (CJNG). The diversion reached $800 million annually, and the effect was devastating: 45% of official weapons ended up in criminal hands. The

State not only failed to contain the organization, but also equipped it with a powerful arsenal, logistics, and intelligence. In practice, law enforcement became unwitting suppliers—or direct accomplices—of one of the most violent organizations on the continent.

Colombia (2022): Police and Gulf Clan, a lethal alliance

The collusion between sectors of the National Police and the Gulf Clan represented an estimated embezzlement of $120 million. But the true impact was not measured in money, but in lives: 28,000 homicides were linked to covert operations where the same anti-drug force protected shipments and executed rivals. The line between the supposed "fight against drugs" and the strengthening of drug trade became blurred until it disappeared, consolidating the image of a state captured from within.

Honduras (2024): " Narco-planes " and the privatization of the air

narco-planes " scandal exposed how agents of the National Anti-Drug Force (FNA) facilitated flights loaded with cocaine in exchange for $60 million. The structural damage was even deeper than the financial: 72% of the country's airports fell under criminal control, transforming Honduras into a virtually privatized air corridor for drug trade. The State, far from safeguarding its sovereignty, became the logistical guarantor of the trafficking.

More than isolated cases: a systemic logic

These episodes cannot be understood as exceptions or "bad apples." They are manifestations of a structural pattern where drug trade infiltrates, corrodes, and ultimately replaces institutions. What emerges is a hybrid model: a cartel-state in which the police repress civilians, judges archive cases, the military guards cargo, and airports become private concessions for organized crime.

The conclusion is inevitable: when the institutions charged with combating drug trade become its main investors, the war on drugs ceases to be a security strategy and becomes a business model. The cost is measured not only in millions of dollars diverted, but also in the loss of citizen trust, the erosion of state legitimacy, and tens of thousands of lives sacrificed in the name of a war that was never against drug trade, but in its favor.

The mechanics of perverse flow

Simplified diagram:

[ANTI-DRUG BUDGET] → [BRIBES] → [NARCO WEAPONS]

Example:

- The citizen pays $100 USD in taxes.
- Of that money, $30 USD is diverted in bribes to military or police commanders.
- With this protection the entry of weapons is ensured:

1 AK-47 costs $450 USD in Texas.

In Mexico it is resold with a criminal margin → $5,000 USD profit.

That rifle can cost the lives of 10 people in a confrontation.

Result: every public dollar invested in "security" is recycled as drug investment, generating 50 times more criminal value.

The mechanics of perverse flow: from tax to drug rifle

The cycle of corruption that runs through the "war on drugs" can be summed up in a brutal equation: every public dollar spent on security is multiplied as criminal profit.

Step 1. The origin: the citizen as an involuntary investor

It all begins with ordinary citizens, who pay taxes with the expectation of security, justice, and stability. However, a significant portion of that budget—on average, 30% in bribes and embezzlement, according to Transparency International (2023)—is absorbed by corrupt military, police, and political leaders. What should protect society ends up lubricating criminal networks.

Step 2. Bribery as investment insurance

Bribery is not an expense, but rather operational insurance for cartels. It guarantees:

- Cargo protection at customs and highways.
- Judicial impunity in case of arrest.
- Privileged information on military operations.

In this way, the same resources that the State allocates to "fighting" drug trade end up financing its logistics.

Step 3. Weaponizing bribery

With this protection, the routes are open to the massive entry of weapons. A prime example is the Russian AK-47 or its American AR-15 variant:

- Price in Texas: $450 USD.
- Criminal price in Mexico: $5,000 USD.
- Profit margin: 1.011%.

That rifle isn't just a weapon of war: it's a criminal profit-making machine. It's estimated that each weapon in the hands of a cartel can result in up to 10 deaths in confrontations, kidnappings, or executions.

Step 4. The criminal multiplication of value

If we follow the flow of a citizen who pays $100 USD in taxes:

- $30 USD is diverted into bribes.
- Those $30 ensure the entry of weapons with margins of thousands of dollars.
- In a matter of days, that "investment" multiplies to generate 50 times more criminal value.

The result is perverse: taxes, instead of buying security, buy insecurity. Society unwittingly finances the very machinery that destroys it.

Historical comparison: from the "royal fifth" to the drug tax

This mechanism is reminiscent of the colonial "royal fifth" (the 20% mining tax that ended up concentrated in the Spanish Crown). The difference is that, in the narco-trafficking model, the citizen tribute is transformed not into imperial palaces, but into rifles, corpses, and devastated communities.

Conclusion: The State as an investor in crime

The mechanics of the perverse flow show that the war on drugs is financially unsustainable: every dollar invested in public security is recycled as criminal profit, multiplying violence. Instead of weakening the enemy, the state becomes its main capitalist partner.

The collapse of legitimacy

The truly devastating impact of the war on drugs is not measured only in deaths or tons of cocaine seized, but in the erosion of state legitimacy. What is collapsing is not only security: it is trust in the social pact that should sustain institutions.

1. Crisis of social trust: the broken contract

When a citizen sees that the military and police—supposedly guardians of the law—end up supplying weapons to drug traffickers, the social contract is shattered. Paying taxes and paying the extortion fee become morally and functionally the same: in both cases, the money goes to support the apparatus of violence that oppresses them. The State is no longer perceived as a protector and is instead viewed as just another cartel in uniform. This phenomenon fuels political apathy and the normalization of illegality: if the State doesn't protect, why comply?

2. Zombie institutions: bureaucracies that simulate life

Anti-drug agencies are transformed into zombie institutions: bodies that continue to move, issuing statements and reporting seizures, but which have lost their original essence. What they present as "results" (tons seized, drug lords captured) is only the official accounting, while beneath them a parallel criminal accounting system operates: agreed shipments, cleared routes, and channeled bribes. Drug traffickers don't destroy these institutions; they parasitize them, using them as a facade of legality. The paradox is brutal: every successful operation is, in many cases, a covert negotiation.

3. Inverted geopolitics: international aid as drug fuel

The collapse is not only local, but global. International aid—Plan Colombia, the Mérida Initiative, and US military cooperation—instead of dismantling criminal structures, ended up fueling corruption on a regional scale. Black Hawk helicopters , assault rifles, and radars donated with international public funds became part of the drug cartel's inventory through diversion, theft, or direct sales by corrupt officials. The logic was reversed: the "war" didn't reduce criminal power; it institutionalized it in a transnational network.

The result: a State degraded to a simulation

When citizen trust evaporates, institutions are devoid of purpose, and international cooperation becomes the raw material for crime, what remains is a state reduced to a semblance of legality. The collapse of legitimacy is the ultimate triumph of drug trade: it no longer needs to challenge the state, because it has become its unwilling partner and, at times, its perfect mask.

Critical Synthesis

Institutional erosion reveals that the so-called war on drug trade has ceased to be a classic confrontation—state versus crime—and has become a hybrid enterprise where the boundaries between legality and illegality are blurring. In practice, a criminal joint venture has emerged in which each actor plays a specific role:

- **The cartels provide** astronomical profits generated by extortion, drug trade, and money laundering.
- **Corrupt governments** provide legal cover, manipulate statistics, and privileged access to weapons, vehicles, and public budgets.
- **Civil societies become** the big losers: they pay with taxes that are recycled into bribes and with lives lost in an endless cycle of violence.

The result is not a partially captured state, but rather a model of mafia-like governance, where drug trade is not a parasite that corrupts the system, but rather a strategic partner that uses it to maximize efficiency and minimize risk.

As a researcher from *the Global Initiative summarizes Against Transnational Organized Crime:*

"In Latin America, drug trade doesn't corrupt the state; it manages it through outsourcing."

This formula explains the region's paradox: the more money is invested in security, the more consolidated criminal power becomes. What collapses is not the bullets or the strategies, but the very legitimacy of the State, reduced to a provider of resources for a business that devours the citizens it claims to protect.

5.4 Lessons from Colombia/Mexico: Manual of Failure

COMPARATIVE BALANCE (Universidad de los Andes, 2024):

The assessment of two decades of dogmatic application of the "war on drugs" model in Colombia and Mexico reveals not mere tactical errors, but a textbook strategic failure. A comparative study by the University of the Andes (2024) demonstrates that both countries, despite their different contexts, implemented the same failed playbook with catastrophic precision, obtaining almost identical results:

atrocious human devastation and a paradoxical strengthening of the very criminal structures they were intended to eradicate. This is not a simple miscalculation; it is evidence of a doctrine founded on erroneous premises.

The Failed Playbook: Three Core Strategies and Their Disastrous Results

The obsession with three pillars—forced eradication, decapitation of leaders, and extradition—proved to be a driving force in perpetuating violence.

1. Forced Eradication: Burning Money, Not Crops

The Strategy: Attack supply at its weakest and most visible link: the farmer. In Colombia, through aerial spraying with glyphosate; in Mexico, through manual eradication.

The Cost: In Colombia, $1.2 million was spent per hectare sprayed, an exorbitant cost that drained resources that could have been allocated to alternative development.

The Perverse Result: Far from reducing the productive base, illicit crops in Colombia grew by 48%. The strategy ignored the fundamental law of the drug economy: the " balloon paradox." "Balloon effect ". By putting pressure on one area, production simply shifts to a more remote area of greater ecological and social value. Fortunes were spent poisoning lands and displacing communities to avoid affecting global supply.

2. The Decapitation of Cartels (" Kingpin") Strategy "): Fragment to Multiply

The Strategy: Create organizational chaos by capturing or eliminating the leaders ("heads") of criminal organizations, in the hope that they will collapse.

The Quantitative "Success": Mexico captured or eliminated 120 high-profile criminal leaders.

The Perverse Result: Far from weakening crime, this strategy was the greatest catalyst for violence. The fragmentation of the large cartels (such as the Sinaloa or Gulf Cartel) gave way to a myriad of warring cells (the Jalisco New Generation Cartel, the Northeast Cartel, etc.) that fiercely dispute territory in much more bloody local wars. This resulted in a 140% increase in violence in Mexico. The "decapitation" didn't kill the monster; it cut off its head, and it regenerated ten more.

3. Extradition: Exporting the Problem, Not Solving It

The Strategy: Dismantle the kingpins' operations from within U.S. maximum-security prisons, depriving them of their operational leadership.

The Figure: Colombia extradited 1,200 drug lords; Mexico extradited 350.

The Perverse Result: Extradition became a ritual of corporate promotion. By eliminating the old guard, the professionalization of organizations accelerated. Younger, more violent, and more digitalized leaders took control. Far from dismantling the structures, they became more agile, decentralized, and difficult to combat. The number of criminal groups skyrocketed by 300%.

The Final Account: A Macabre Accounting of Wasted Lives and Resources

The human and economic cost of following this manual is unparalleled in obscenity:

Economic Expenditure:

- **Colombia:** Burned $200 billion in two decades.
- **Mexico:** Burned $150 billion in 18 years.

Human Cost:

- **Colombia:** Half a million dead.
- **Mexico:** 450,000 dead and more than 100,000 missing.

The Failure Equation, in cold numbers:

- In Mexico, the strategy had an obscene opportunity cost: for every homicide the model was intended to prevent, $333,000 was spent. Money that, if invested in health, education, or rural development, would have had a real impact on security.
- In Colombia, the capture of each senior drug lord unleashed a wave of forced recruitment equivalent to 1,000 children. The strategy demonstrated that crime's regenerative capacity is practically infinite, fueled by a bottomless pit of poverty and exclusion.

Strategic Conclusion: The Inescapable Lesson

Colombia and Mexico serve as the two most costly large-scale experiments in history in failed security policies. The lesson is unequivocal and devastating:

The "war on drugs" model is a categorical error. It is a self-destructive strategy that drains state resources, structurally strengthens the enemy it seeks to destroy, and produces as its only exportable result a humanitarian catastrophe of historic proportions.

Eradication, decapitation, and extradition tactics are not solutions; they are symptoms of a strategic myopia that confuses violence with the real power of these organizations. The cartels' true power lies not in an individual leader or a poppy field, but in their ability to integrate into the global economy through money laundering, to co-opt state institutions, and to offer a parallel economy where the state is absent.

Persisting in this model isn't stubborn; it's complicit. The only valid lesson this manual of failure offers is the urgent need for a radical paradigm shift: abandoning war and redirecting all resources toward state-building, social justice, market regulation, and harm reduction. Any other path is to sign the condemnation of the next 500,000 victims.

SUMMARY: THE ARITHMETIC OF STUPIDITY

The arithmetic of stupidity

The so-called "war on drugs" can be summed up as a perverse equation where the cost is borne by the State and the profit is multiplied in the hands of drug traffickers.

The prohibition policy, which consumes $1.5 trillion annually globally, barely achieves a 0.3% reduction in consumption, while cartel profits have grown by 1,600%. Militarization, which in Mexico and Colombia totaled $270 billion, did not eliminate a single cartel, but it did allow criminal groups to expand their territorial control by 300%.

The extraditions are equally absurd: each case costs $12,000, but 98% of extradited leaders are replaced within 72 hours, resulting in a 450% fragmentation of criminal activity and an even greater diversification of illicit economies. Finally, crop spraying with chemicals like glyphosate, at a rate of $6,000 per hectare, not only fails to eradicate the plantations: crops have increased by 32%, and with them, prices have risen by 200%.

Taken together, the numbers show that each state "strategy" is actually a covert subsidy to criminal enterprise.

Emblematic case: the Calderón effect (Mexico)

The most brutal example of this structural failure is Mexico after the militarization that began in 2006.

- In that year, the initial investment was $7 billion annually.
- By 2010, the "strategy" had left 60,000 dead and 12,000 missing.
- In 2012, the cartels grew from six to 32 factions, and their profits doubled, from $25 billion to $60 billion.
- In 2024, the legacy is devastating: $150 billion spent, 300,000 dead, and 98,000 missing.

The forensic conclusion is unappealable: every dollar invested by the State generated $8.50 in profits for the cartels.

War, presented as a solution, was nothing more than the most profitable business ever designed for organized crime.

ANALYSIS OF LEARNING FROM FAILURE

The so-called "war on drugs" is not just a strategic mistake: it is the greatest economic and social disaster of the 21st century. Its logic functions as a regressive tax where the poor pay in blood while bankers, military contractors, and pharmaceutical corporations reap multi-billion-dollar profits.

The data is clear: prohibition increases drug profits sixfold; militarization fragments cartels, but at the cost of tripling violence; and persecuting farmers only attacks the weakest links in the chain, ignoring the fact that 0.1% of drug lords account for 92% of the profits from the illegal market.

In this context, the solution cannot be "more war." The evidence points to only one viable path: defunding terror. This means legalizing and regulating markets, investing in rural and urban communities, and prioritizing public health policies over criminal punishment.

The precedent is clear: Portugal demonstrated that harm reduction is 50 times cheaper than armed pursuit, while Uruguay reduced homicides by 52% in five years after regulating cannabis.

Instead, insisting on prohibition reproduces a vicious cycle where every dollar invested in security ends up being converted into more power for the mafias.

The vicious circle of drug trade

The flow chart starkly illustrates the perverse logic of the war on drugs, a self-reinforcing cycle that has proven to be as costly as it is ineffective. Each stage generates the next, in an upward spiral of violence and criminal profits:

BAN (✖)

The decision to prohibit drugs instead of regulating them artificially created an underground market. In economics, what is prohibited becomes more profitable because scarcity translates into higher prices.

1. **PRICES ↑ (+500%)**

The cost of cocaine, marijuana, and heroin has multiplied exponentially in consumer markets (the U.S. and Europe), not because of their intrinsic value, but because of the "risk" associated with trafficking. In New York, for example, a kilo of cocaine went from $25,000 USD in 1971 to more than $150,000 USD in 2024.

1. **NARCO PROFITS ↑ (+1,600%)**

What was a failure for states was a blessing for the cartels: global drug trade profits soared from $100 billion in the 1970s to $1.7 trillion today. Prohibition served as an indirect subsidy for organized crime.

1. **MILITARIZATION (◈)**

Faced with these enormous profits, the state's response has been to deploy armies, helicopters, and heavy weapons. However, militarization does not destroy the criminal structure: it fragments, disperses, and multiplies it.

1. **CARTEL FRAGMENTATION (↑ violence)**

Each captured drug lord opens the door for three new emerging groups. In Mexico, the number of gangs has increased from six large organizations in 2006 to more than 32 by 2024. Competition for territory drives homicide rates higher and turns entire regions into war zones.

1. MORE ANTI-DRUG BUDGET (◈ → ◈)

Rising violence becomes a justification for increased military and police budgets. But a significant portion of these funds ends up diverted into corruption, fueling crime once again. It's a negative feedback loop, where failure is rewarded with more money.

Conclusion of visual resources

The graph shows that every dollar invested in prohibiting and militarization becomes fuel for the criminal engine. The only way to break this cycle is not to continue feeding it, but to defuse it at its roots through regulated legalization, social investment, and harm reduction policies.

In other words: prohibiting multiplexes, regulating deactivates.

"No one in history has ever shot at supply and demand. Not even with machine guns."

— Milton Friedman, Nobel Prize in Economics 1976

"The war on drugs is a foregone conclusion: you fight smoke with fire, and in the process you feed the monster."

— Dr. Laura Atuesta, crime economist (CIDE)

ECONOMIC ANALYSIS OF THE ANATOMY OF FAILURE

The so-called "war on drugs" has not only failed in its stated objectives, but has also followed the laws of thermodynamics of corruption: invested (economic) energy is not destroyed, but transformed, strengthening the very system it was intended to annihilate. A cold analysis of the figures reveals the anatomy of this colossal failure.

1. Economic Absurdity: Investing More to Obtain Worse Results

U.S. Government Accountability Office (GAO), the country invests $35 billion annually in the fight against drugs, an astronomical figure allocated to interdiction, international operations, and incarceration. However, the tangible result is a 22% increase in the consumption of illicit substances. This figure does not represent a simple miscalculation; it is proof of a failed model. Supply adapts, diversifies, and becomes more efficient under pressure, inflating the costs of the war while the core problem not only persists but grows. It is the equivalent of pouring money into a bottomless pit, unwittingly financing the very resilience of drug trade.

2. Market Distortion: The "Iron Law" of Prohibition

State pressure acts as a catalyst that distorts the rules of the criminal market. The testimony of a retired Colombian general puts it bluntly: "We would capture one boss... and three new ones would appear, financed with the same money that was supposed to fight them." This phenomenon, known as the "hydra effect," demonstrates how the dismantling of a group creates a power vacuum that is immediately filled by more violent and decentralized factions. Anti-drug policy, far from weakening the business, eliminates the least efficient actors and strengthens the most brutal and corrupt. Taxpayer money, by financing this war, indirectly becomes the seed capital that finances the fragmentation and evolution of the cartels, increasing violence and instability.

3. The Responsibility and Moral Consequences of the Consumer

The economic cycle of drug trade closes with demand. The DEA (Drug Enforcement The U.S. Department of Agriculture (DPA) estimates that 84% of the cocaine circulating in the United States comes from cartels whose operations are based on practices of terror and inhumane exploitation. This is not an abstract statistic; it translates into the enslavement of children for cultivation and surveillance, massacres to control transit territories, and the corruption of institutions that should protect citizens. Every dollar spent by a consumer on the streets of any Western city is a dollar that flows directly into this ecosystem of violence. The dissociation between the act of consumption and its catastrophic geopolitical and human consequences is the cartels' greatest propaganda triumph.

Conclusion: A Model That Feeds Its Own Failure

The analysis reveals a closed-loop system of economic perversity:

- Taxpayers found a costly war.
- These funds, leaked through corruption, arm and enriched the cartels.
- The resulting violence justifies increasing the war budget.
- Consumers complete the cycle, providing the demand that makes the entire business profitable.

This conflict-producing machine benefits bureaucrats, arms manufacturers, and criminals alike, while societies on both sides of the border pay the price in lives, security, and dignity. "War" is, in reality, the business itself.

FINAL ANALYSIS

A REVIEW OF THE HISTORY and effects of the war on drugs confirms an insurmountable paradox: what was designed as a policy of control resulted in a mechanism of expansion. Each axis of strategy prohibition, militarization, pursuit of drug lords, international cooperation—did not weaken drug trade but rather strengthened it by generating perverse incentives. Instead of reducing supply or demand, what multiplied were profit margins, corruption networks, and systemic violence.

The failure isn't technical, it's structural. It's not that states have lacked capacity or resources, but that the model itself is designed to produce the results we are now experiencing: concentration of wealth in criminal hands, eroded institutions, communities trapped in a cycle of terror, and a global financial system that operates as a necessary accomplice to money laundering. A comparative analysis of Mexico and Colombia confirms this: billions of dollars invested in helicopters, fumigations, and troops only perpetuated the war and multiplied the death toll.

The assessment is as overwhelming as it is uncomfortable: the so-called war on drugs is not a failed policy, it is a policy serving hidden interests. It serves the arms industry that supplies both sides; the banks that launder money; the political elites that wield violence as electoral capital; and an international system that tolerates the perpetuation of this illicit economy because it fuels the very machinery of global capitalism.

What's at stake, then, is not just the effectiveness of a security strategy, but the very meaning of the social contract. A state that turns its citizens into cannon fodder while its institutions indirectly finance the enemy has lost not only the battle, but also its legitimacy. The war on drugs exposes the fragility of Latin American democracies, where the line between state and crime becomes indistinguishable and where communities discover that paying taxes or extortion is, in essence, the same transaction.

Thus, understanding the anatomy of failure is not an academic exercise: it is a condition of survival. Only by recognizing the economic, institutional, and social dimensions of the disaster can we imagine a different path. And that path involves abandoning the mirage that more repression will bring more peace, and beginning to think in terms of defunding, regulation, and productive alternatives that compete with the logic of drug trade.

The war on drugs has lasted for more than half a century because it serves useful purposes for those who wage it. The historical challenge is to break that cycle, dismantle the mirage of war, and open up the possibility of a future where life is worth more than the profitability of a rifle or a shipment of cocaine.

PART VI: THE LOGIC OF MODERN SLAVERY

The drug trade phenomenon is often described in superficial economic terms: an "illegal market" that creates jobs, produces wealth, and competes with the formal economy. However, this view is misleading and even dangerous. Far from serving as an alternative for social mobility for excluded sectors, the drug structure reproduces—with modern tools—the most archaic logic of domination: slavery and feudalism.

The following chapter does not address drug trade as simply organized crime or a parallel business to global capitalism, but as an economic and political regime in itself, sustained by extraction, violence, and fear. Its machinery is not sustained by labor contracts, social rights, or economic mobility, but by the absolute subordination of thousands of men, women, and entire communities. In this sense, more than a black market, it constitutes a political economy of servitude.

The comparison with feudalism and colonial economies, it is not a rhetorical device, but a structural correspondence. As in a slave plantation or a colonial mine, a tiny elite concentrates immeasurable fortunes, while a massive and disposable base bears the weight of risk, violence, and exploitation. Wealth neither circulates nor generates development: it escapes in the form of laundered money to tax havens, luxurious mansions, or speculative investments, leaving behind devastated territories, forced displacement, and entire generations trapped in a cycle of poverty and fear.

The chapter also shows that the true "fuel" of this economy is not the drug itself, but the ability to administer mechanisms of social control through fear. Performative violence, territorial control, and the normalization of brutality constitute authentic political technologies that transform the cartel into a parallel state: regulator of life and death, of the local economy, and even of community relations.

In this logic, even the apparent rewards—the quick cash, the luxury SUV, the gold-plated gun—are merely golden bars of a cage that locks recruits in perpetual servitude. There is no real advancement, nor possible resignation; only three ways out: prison, death, or eternal submission.

This chapter, therefore, invites us to dismantle the narrative of drug trade as an "economic option" and understand it for what it truly is: a system of modern slavery and extreme concentration of wealth, whose impact transcends the criminal to become part of the long history of mechanisms of human exploitation.

Far from the romanticized vision of " narco-laboratories " or "alternative jobs," the drug trade industry does not operate as an informal economy offering opportunities, but rather as a 21st-century slave system. Its operation responds to a political economy of terror, designed to maximize control and the extraction of wealth through violence, fear, and dependence. Unlike other illegal markets, cartels do not generate social mobility or networks for economic advancement: they reproduce structures of forced servitude, where human life is treated as a fungible resource.

6.1. From Pyramid to Fiefdom: The Hyper-Concentration of Criminal Wealth

THE DRUG TRADE ECONOMY does not respond to the capitalist logic of open markets, competition, and social mobility. Its structure is much older and more brutal: a feudal-extractivist model, where a tiny elite accumulates unimaginable fortunes at the expense of a massive base of workers subjugated by violence, debt, and fear.

Stately dome: the "patrons" of the fief

At the top is a tiny minority—less than 0.1% of a cartel's members—who control trafficking routes, logistical infrastructure, and the monopoly on violence. They are the contemporary equivalent of medieval feudal lords, empowered to impose war taxes, recruit private armies, and dictate the rules of life and death in the territories they dominate.

- Joaquín "El Chapo" Guzmán accumulated more than $14 billion USD in annual profits, according to the DEA, while his hitmen received only between $400 and $800 USD per month.
- This imbalance turns the bosses into true "local kings," whose wealth rivals that of legal corporations and whose authority surpasses that of the state itself in vast regions.

Servile base: disposable labor

The vast majority of those involved in this criminal economy are not entrepreneurs or even wage earners in the modern sense, but rather precariously employed servants. These include peasants who grow opium poppies or coca under duress, young people who act as "hawks" for miserable wages, or hitmen who risk their lives for incomes below the minimum wage.

- The replacement rate is brutal: a hitman costs around $15,000

USD a year in payments, but killing or replacing him can cost as little as $1,000 USD. From a business perspective, a worker is cheaper dead than keeping him alive in the long term.

- Their existence is marked by unpayable debts (clothing, weapons, drugs), which turns them into modern-day slaves, trapped in a system of perpetual servitude.

Extractive relationship: the wealth that never trickles down

The distribution of income is the clearest evidence of the feudal nature of drug trade. DEA studies and calculations based on the trial of "El Chapo" indicate that 90–95% of profits remain in the hands of less than 1% of the members, while the remaining 99% receive only 2–5% of the total.

- This pattern is no different from the slave plantations of the 19th century, where the owners concentrated up to 90% of the profits and the slaves barely survived on food and shelter.
- In practical terms, the wealth generated by cartels does not energize communities: it does not create sustainable jobs or public infrastructure, but rather extracts value and concentrates it in offshore accounts, luxury properties, and speculative assets.

Social consequences: structural devastation

Drug trafficking doesn't build development: it parasitizes communities until they are empty. Where it establishes itself:

- "Taxes" are imposed through widespread extortion.
- Forced displacement occurs: entire villages are expelled to open logistical corridors.
- Traditional local economies—agriculture, commerce, trades—collapse, replaced by a war economy controlled by violence.

- The population is trapped in an intergenerational cycle of poverty, fear and dependency.

Synthesis

Cartels are not "criminal enterprises" in the style of modern corporations, but rather feudal fiefdoms with a lordly structure. Their leaders function like feudal lords with private armies, monopolizing wealth and exercising armed sovereignty over communities that are reduced to the status of vassals. The narco economy is an inverted mirror of extreme capitalism: it produces neither mobility nor competition, but absolute servitude and concentration.

6.2. The Metallurgy of Fear: Forging Invisible Chains

IN THE DRUG TRADE ECOSYSTEM, the legal currency is not the dollar or the peso, but fear. This is not wielded in an improvised manner, but as a carefully designed instrument of power, functioning simultaneously as an economy, language, and technology of social control. Fear not only disciplines: it forges invisible chains that bind entire communities to the logic of perpetual obedience.

1. Performative terror.

Public executions, bodies hanging from bridges, clandestine graves, and narco-banners are much more than episodes of extreme violence: they are theatrical acts of political communication. They constitute a "marketing of terror" that sends an unequivocal message: disobedience has an unaffordable cost. Violence ceases to be a means to domination and becomes a spectacle of domination. Each exposed corpse serves as a pamphlet: a reminder to everyone—victims, rivals, authorities, and civilians—that the only possible option is submission.

2. Total territorial control.

Drug trafficking isn't limited to drug trade: it governs entire communities. Cartels impose traffic schedules, curfews, and "war taxes," dictating who can enter or leave a community. Patron saint festivals, trade routes, and even the daily lives of residents are subject to a regime of criminal authorization. In many territories, the state is absent, infiltrated, or complicit, turning cartels into de facto governments, capable of replacing institutions in the management of life and death.

3. Normalization of violence.

Constant exposure to brutality has a corrosive effect on the collective psyche. What would otherwise be unbearable becomes part of the everyday landscape. Violence ceases to be exceptional and becomes the norm, establishing a culture of resigned submission. Resistance seems not only impossible but irrational: how can one confront a power that dominates not only with weapons, but with symbols, rumors, and omnipresent fear? The result is a population domesticated by terror, which incorporates violence into its daily life as if it were inevitable.

Together, these three mechanisms forge a system of modern slavery where the chains are not of iron, but of fear. Control of the body is ensured through control of the mind and control of territory. In this context, violence is not just a means of illicit profit: it is the central political technology that allows drug trade to perpetuate itself as a parallel order of domination.

In the drug trade ecosystem, the true legal tender is not the dollar or the peso: it's fear. This is not wielded in an improvised or chaotic manner, but as an instrument of systematic power, designed with surgical precision. It functions simultaneously as an economy (because it generates profit), a language (because it communicates political messages), and a technology of social control (because it disciplines bodies and minds). In this system, fear not only represses: it creates invisible chains that bind entire communities to a logic of perpetual obedience.

---

1. Performative terror: the theater of cruelty

Public executions, bodies hanging from bridges, heads left in squares, clandestine graves, and narco-banners are not isolated episodes of barbarism, but rather acts of political communication. They constitute the "marketing of terror": scenes carefully choreographed to send an unequivocal message.

- Each exposed corpse is a visual pamphlet announcing that disobedience has an incalculable cost.
- Crime is no longer clandestine: it is displayed with brutal scenery, as a public spectacle.
- Violence doesn't just kill: it speaks, warns, and persuades. In this sense, it becomes a language as clear as a written law.

The result is a theater of cruelty in which the message transcends the specific victim. The goal is not just to eliminate an enemy, but to sow terror in a hundred witnesses. Thus, violence ceases to be a means and becomes a spectacle of collective domination.

2. Total territorial control: the sovereignty of fear

Drug traffickers don't limit themselves to drug trade; they manage entire communities as if they were modern fiefdoms. Where the state is absent, infiltrated, or subservient, the cartels exercise de facto sovereignty:

- They impose curfews and control who enters or leaves a town.
- They charge "war taxes" (extortion) to merchants, transporters and producers.
- They regulate social life: from patron saint festivals to local markets, everything requires authorization.
- They monitor the population through networks of hawks, creating a total surveillance system.

In this regime, residents are not just governed: they are managed as resources. The entire community lives under an inverted social contract, where security is not provided by the state, but by forced obedience to criminal power. The line between "citizen" and "subject" disappears: people cease to belong to a democratic republic and become part of a drug fiefdom.

3. Normalization of violence: psychological domestication

Perhaps the most devastating effect is not on the dead, but on the living. Constant exposure to brutality generates a phenomenon of psychological acclimatization: what would otherwise be intolerable becomes part of everyday life.

- Children grow up playing at being hitmen, naturalizing violence as a social aspiration.
- The inhabitants learn to remain silent, not to look, not to ask questions, because resistance seems not only impossible, but irrational.
- Collective resignation takes hold as a form of survival: silence replaces protest.

Thus, violence ceases to be the exception and becomes the norm. In the words of a community leader from Guerrero: "We no longer live here; we only survive fear."

Summary: The invisible engineering of terror

The metallurgy of fear is the process by which cartels transform violence into a tool of parallel government. Control of the body is ensured through control of the mind; control of the territory is perpetuated through the forced obedience of its inhabitants.

Together, these three mechanisms—performative terror, territorial control, and the normalization of violence—constitute a system of modern slavery without physical chains, where obedience is imposed not by legal contract, but by the threat of extermination. Violence, more than a means of illicit profit, emerges as the central political technology that allows drug trade to perpetuate itself as an order of domination parallel to the state.

6.3. The Rotten Golden Cage: The Impossibility of Renunciation

THE NOTION OF "RESIGNING" from a cartel is a mirage. In this feudal-criminal order, membership is not an employment contract or voluntary association, but a perpetual servitude. The cage that encloses members may be lined with momentary luxuries—cars, guns, quick cash—but inside, the logic is one of absolute slavery: entering is easy; leaving is a death sentence.

1. **Perpetual debts.**

The first lock is economic. Many recruits are lured with advances of weapons, drugs, clothing, or cash that chain them to a system of unpayable debts. Each "advance" expense is compounded by impossible-to-cover interest. This mechanism reproduces a debt servitude, inherited from the colonial hacienda or the Porfiriato, where the day laborer could never settle his bill at the local grocery store. Here, the hitman, the hawk, or the peasant farmer are trapped in an impossible calculation: they always owe more than they receive.

2. Knowledge as condemnation.

Anyone who enters the criminal network acquires sensitive information: trafficking routes, safe houses, names of bosses, communication codes. This knowledge turns each member into an operational risk. In legal business logic, resignation implies confidentiality. In criminal logic, resignation is equivalent to potential betrayal. That's why the maxim "the only way out is death or imprisonment" isn't a cliché, but a formal human resource management policy for drug traffickers. The body of the defector becomes the guarantee of eternal silence.

3. Collective punishment.

The third lock is emotional and communal. Desertion is not paid for individually, but collectively. Fleeing doesn't mean saving oneself, but rather condemning one's children, siblings, or parents to retribution. Drug traffickers turn family ties into mechanisms of internal surveillance, where love and loyalty become instruments of slavery. Those who try to escape not only risk their lives but also sign the death sentence of their entire emotional network.

4. The mirage of promotion.

Finally, the system offers symbolic rewards—the golden gun, the luxury SUV, access to women, the ephemeral respect of the community—that build a rotten gilded cage. They appear to be privileges, but in reality, they are shiny chains that make escape more difficult. The hitman with luxuries is not a free man: he is a prisoner caged with gold-plated bars.

Together, these mechanisms turn life within the cartel into a contract without exit. There is no resignation, no retirement, no return to civilian life. There are only three possible destinations: the graveyard, prison, or permanent submission. Drug trafficking, thus, perfects a form of contemporary slavery that uses debt, secrets, affection, and poisoned luxuries as its invisible chains.

6.4. The New Warehouses of Humanity: Parallels with Extractive Colonialism

CARTELS ARE NOT SIMPLY "criminal enterprises"; they are machines of human and territorial extraction that reproduce, in new forms, the same logic that characterized colonial slave economies. If the sugar plantations of the Caribbean or the mines of Potosí in the Viceroyalty of Peru were the "warehouses" of enslaved humanity in past centuries, today drug routes, clandestine laboratories, and dominated plazas fulfill the same function: spaces of extreme exploitation where the human body is just another resource, subjected to a political economy of death.

1. Person as a disposable tool

On the colonial plantation, the slave was considered a "piece" or "workhorse"; among drug dealers, the hitman, the hawk, or the mule were designated as "hot," "disposable," or "workhorses." The language reveals the logic: their value lies not in their humanity, but in their ability to transport, kill, or guard merchandise.

- A hitman killed in a confrontation is an affordable cost, since replacing him costs less than keeping him alive.
- The body of the cocaine mule is worth less than the cargo carried in the stomach or attached to the skin.
- A young man recruited in a marginalized neighborhood has such a short lifespan that his useful life for the cartel is measured in months, not years.

The equation is brutal: the commodity matters more than the bearer. As in colonialism, the person becomes an "instrument of biological production," disposable once their function is fulfilled.

2. Extraction to the point of collapse: the criminal enclave economy

The narco model reproduces classic extractivist logic: it doesn't seek sustainability, but rather maximum profit in minimum time.

- A square is squeezed to the point of saturation: extortion, kidnapping, control of businesses, drug monopoly.
- When a territory collapses due to violence or state intervention, criminal capital migrates to another "virgin" area, repeating the cycle.
- Entire communities are razed and abandoned, like exhausted mines, leaving behind displacement, dispossession, and a devastated social landscape.

This pattern is reminiscent of the colonial enclave economy: extracting gold, silver, or sugar without investing in local development, only in extraction. The territory is not inhabited: it is exploited and abandoned.

3. Systematic dehumanization: the ideology of exploitation

Drug trafficking, like colonialism, requires stripping victims of their human condition so that mass exploitation is tolerable for those who practice it.

- Narco language—"hawk," "mule," "hot"—is an ideological device: it reduces people to animals or instruments.
- This objectification is no coincidence: it is the mental lubricant that allows thousands of poor young people to be used as cannon fodder.
- In colonial times, slaves were classified as "pieces" in accounting inventories; today, hitmen are statistics in criminal records.

In this way, the system naturalizes extreme violence and turns it into routine, justifying the annihilation of the others under the premise that they were never fully human.

Conclusion: Drug trafficking as a miniature totalitarian regime

The cartel is not a business in the modern sense, but rather a local totalitarian political regime. Its power comes not from consent or a social contract, but from the ability to inflict harm, monopolize violence, and present itself as the guarantor of extortionate "security" in a state vacuum.

Understanding this modern slavery logic is crucial: it debunks the narrative that drug trade is an "economic option" for the poor. In reality, it is the option of total exploitation, where the individual obtains merely a temporary extension of their life in exchange for becoming a cog in a death machine that concentrates wealth in the hands of a tiny elite.

If slave colonialism marked centuries of plunder, drug trade reproduces that same logic in the 21st century: new warehouses of humanity, where life is worth less than merchandise and the future is mortgaged in service of an economy of blood.

SLAVERY LOGIC (Focus: Concentration of Wealth)

The cartel's operating system does not represent a distortion of capitalism, but rather the resurrection of a feudal model of production adapted to the 21st century. It is an economic structure designed for the maximum extraction and concentration of wealth, where the productive base—made up of hitmen, farmers, thugs, and money launderers—is not a working class, but a mass of modern serfs trapped in a cycle of dependency, violence, and perpetual poverty. Wealth is not distributed; it is siphoned off to the top through brutally efficient mechanisms of exploitation.

1. The Pyramid of Criminal Inequality: Concentration at the Top

The distribution of profits within a cartel follows a curve of inequality that dwarfs that of any country or corporation in the world.

The 0.01% of the Top (The "Feudal Lords"): This tiny elite—the leaders and their closest financial associates—concentrates between 80% and 85% of all profits. Their income is derived from money laundering, investment in the formal economy, and the capture of public contracts. They live in absolute secrecy, enjoying assets measured in billions of dollars.

The 99.9% of the Base (The "Servants"): The vast majority survive on less than 5% of the total resources generated. A low-ranking hitman earns between $300 and $800 USD per month; a grower or "halcón" (vigilante) earns much less. This subsistence wage does not compensate for the risk of life and the high opportunity costs (school dropout, psychological trauma, life expectancy of ~35 years). They generate enormous value but capture a tiny portion of it.

Illustration: The wholesale value of a kilo of cocaine (~$30,000 USD) is equivalent to a hitman's combined 10 years' salary. The disconnect between productivity and remuneration is complete.

2. The Replacement Rate: The Economics of Human Waste

The financial logic of the cartel's values human life in purely utilitarian and replacement cost terms.

Maintenance Cost vs. Replacement Cost:

- Keeping a hitman for a year (salary, basic food, basic weapon): ~ $15,000 USD.
- Replace (recruit and train a new member, often through coercion or deception): ~$1,000 USD.

Operational Conclusion: It is 15 times cheaper to replace a member than to retain them and invest in their well-being. This equation turns life into a disposable asset. The extremely high mortality rate is not a problem for the organization; it is a calculated variable in its business model. The "replacement rate" guarantees a constant flow of new recruits, fueled by poverty and a lack of alternatives, making the organization immune to human attrition.

3. Historical Parallels: 21st Century Plantations

The cartels' economic model structurally reproduces the scheme of 19th-century slave plantations, albeit with modernized operating mechanisms. This comparison is evident in five critical dimensions:

Regarding worker control, slave plantations exercised their dominance through physical chains and brutal surveillance, while contemporary cartels use family coercion, bloodthirsty debts, and territorial control. Both strategies, although different in their execution, share a common objective: suppressing freedom through various mechanisms to guarantee absolute submission.

The distribution of wealth shows patterns of extreme concentration. Plantation owners captured more than 98% of the value generated, while the current criminal elite appropriates more than 85% of the profits. In both cases, wealth is concentrated in the hands of a property-owning elite that controls the means of production.

Labor costs are kept to a minimum in both systems. Plantations allocated approximately 2% of their profits to maintaining slaves, while cartels allocated less than 5% to starvation wages without benefits for their operational base. This logic reflects the fact that investment in "human assets" is reduced to the bare minimum necessary to maintain them productive.

The replacement policy demonstrates the devaluation of human life. Slaves were considered replaceable assets , and their high mortality rate was acceptable, while cartels considered hitmen expendable and operated under a logic where the "replacement rate" was key. In both models, human life was treated as a commodity, not a right.

Finally, both systems depend on a perverse legal framework that protects the operation. Plantations relied on slave laws that protected the owner's "property," while contemporary cartels operate through structural corruption and the imposition of a "narco law" that supplants the state. In both cases, the existing legal system is co-opted or replaced to serve the extractive model.

Case Study (Guerrero, Mexico): Poppy growers receive approximately $150 USD per kilo of raw rubber. The cartel transforms it into heroin and sells it in the U.S. for $80,000 USD/kg. The grower captures only 0.19% of the product's final value—a rate of exploitation that exceeds even the most extractive colonial models.

Conclusion: The Myth of Social Mobility and the Reality of Criminal Feudalism

The popular narrative that drug trade offers "social mobility" is a dangerous mirage. The system is not designed to create prosperity, but to extract and concentrate it.

- **For the Base:** It offers only high-risk survival. There is no career advancement, no capital accumulation, no pensions. The ultimate destination is prison, death, or irreversible trauma.
- **For leadership:** It's the perfect accumulation machine. It concentrates wealth at a minimal social cost, externalizing all the violence and risk to the productive base and society at large.

Cartels are not enterprises that generate development; they are parasitic entities that build their wealth on the maximum exploitation of human beings and territories. They are the modern expression of armed feudalism, where drug lords rule their fiend with impunity, and where the lives of their serfs are worth less than the replacement of a work tool. Understanding this logic of slavery is essential to dismantling the myth that organized crime is a path to progress and to focusing solutions on attacking its mechanisms of wealth extraction and concentration.

ECONOMIC ANALYSIS OF THE LOGIC OF MODERN SLAVERY

Drug trafficking is not simply an illicit market: it is a modern feudal system, where wealth and power are concentrated at the top, while the labor force—hitmen, thugs, and recruits—operates under conditions of extreme exploitation and constant risk.

1. Extreme distribution of wealth.

A drug lord like Ismael "El Mayo" Zambada accumulates approximately $10 billion USD, while his bodyguard or base hitman earns barely $800 USD a month, with an average life expectancy within the organization of 28 years. This gap demonstrates a brutal concentration of capital: 0.01% of the hierarchy controls the vast majority of resources, while 99.9% of the base survives on less than 5%.

2. Historical comparison: mortality and replacement.

The annual mortality rate of sicarii is estimated at 40%, comparable to that of slaves in Roman gold mines, according to Keith Hopkins. This high risk turns recruits into disposable assets, optimized to produce value with minimal investment in their well-being. The logic is simple: replacing a sicarii is cheaper than ensuring their prolonged survival.

3. Perverse financial flow.

The economic value of a child hitman is infinitesimal compared to the business: 1 kg of cocaine can be equivalent to three months of a hitman's salary, provided he is paid fairly. Every death and every new recruit are counted as an investment and return, creating a model where fear and violence are commonplace, and human life becomes an economic commodity.

Conclusion: This system reproduces, in a modern way, the mechanisms of historical slavery: concentration of wealth, high risk to the rank and file, rapid turnover, and maximum exploitation of human resources. The elite benefits from a constant flow of profits while perpetuating a cycle of dependency, violence, and social control that turns entire communities into fiefdoms of economic terror.

EXTREME CONCENTRATION OF WEALTH (Narco Inequality Ratio)

Case study: Sinaloa Cartel (Mexico)

- **Primary source:** Judgment of the trial against Joaquín "El Chapo" Guzmán (Eastern District Court of New York, 2019).
- **Key fact:** The cartel moved $14 billion USD annually according to the DEA (2017).

Real distribution of wealth:

- **Dome (0.1%):** Joaquín Guzmán earned approximately $300 million USD per year (Forbes, 2009).
- **Base (99.9%):** Hitmen, hawks and recruits survived on $400-$800 USD/month (Insight) Crime , 2020).

Inequality Calculation:

- The top 0.1% captured 86% of total profits.
- The base (99.9%) received only 0.02% of the total, showing an extreme imbalance in the distribution of resources.
- This concentration not only reflects accumulated wealth, but also a feudal economic model, where most workers are disposable assets.

Historical parallel to slavery:

- US cotton plantations (1850), 0.1% of the owners accumulated 90% of the wealth, while the slaves only received food and shelter (Bancroft, Slave Trading, 1931).
- The logic is identical: a tiny group controls the majority of resources while the base carries out intensive work in conditions of extreme vulnerability.

Conclusion: The Sinaloa Cartel reproduces a modern feudal exploitation model, where wealth and power are concentrated at the top, and most members of the organization survive in precarious conditions, perpetuating inequality, dependency and structural vulnerability.

Final Analysis: The Logic of Modern Slavery in

Drug Trafficking

THE CHAPTER PRESENTS a powerful and well-founded thesis: drug trade is not an alternative informal economy, but a system of modern slavery operating under a feudal-extractivist logic. Far from being a distortion of capitalism, this system represents the resurrection of an archaic model of domination, but one adapted with brutal precision to the 21st century.

1. **Key Contributions of the Analysis:**

Deconstructing the Myth of "Alternative Employment": The text effectively debunks the romanticized narrative that presents drug trade as a means of social mobility or employment for the marginalized. Instead, it reveals a system of debt servitude and coercion, where the vast majority of participants are "precarious servants" trapped in a cycle of poverty, violence, and early death.

1. **The Feudal Framework as an Analytical Tool**: The comparison with feudalism is not merely metaphorical. The chapter demonstrates how cartels replicate seigneurial power structures:

- A tiny elite (the "feudal lords") that accumulates 85-95% of the wealth.
- A massive base (the "serfs") surviving on crumbs (2-5% of profits) assuming all the risk.
- Absolute territorial control through private armies and the imposition of "taxes" (extortion).
- The replacement of the State as the de facto authority, administering life and death in its fiefdoms.

1. **The Political Economy of Terror:** This chapter goes beyond

traditional economic analysis to argue that the real currency of the system is fear. This is not a byproduct, but a carefully designed central technology of control. "Performative terror," the normalization of violence, and total territorial control are mechanisms that forge psychological chains of perpetual obedience, creating a domesticated population.

2. **The Impossibility of Exit:** The fallacy of "renunciation" is exposed. The system is designed with perverse locks—unpayable debts, knowledge as a mortal sentence, collective punishment of families, and the mirage of luxury—that turn belonging into lifelong servitude, where the only escapes are prison or death.
3. **Disturbing Historical Parallels**: The comparison with colonial slave economies and plantations is compelling and chilling. The central logic is shown to be identical: the dehumanization and objectification of the human being as a disposable resource ("hawk," "mule," "hot"), whose value is less than that of the commodity they transport or protect. The calculated "replacement rate" (it is 15 times cheaper to replace a hitman than to keep him) is the starkest example of this logic.

Conclusion and Final Reflection:

The chapter rightly concludes that cartels are "miniature totalitarian regimes." Their power stems not from the social contract, but from their monopoly on violence and the ability to instill terror. This analysis is crucial because:

- **It demystifies the nature of organized crime:** It presents it not as a business, but as a political-economic system of oppression.
- **He challenges simplistic solutions:** He suggests that

combating drug trade requires much more than police operations; it requires attacking the mechanisms of wealth extraction and concentration, the impunity of the elite, and the conditions of poverty and lack of rule of law that allow this criminal feudalism to flourish.
- **It offers a clear ethical framework:** By defining the system as slavery, it eliminates any moral ambiguity. This isn't about "jobs" or "choices," but about totalitarian exploitation that mortgages the future of entire communities in the service of a parasitic elite.

In essence, this chapter achieves its goal: to provide a robust and critical lens for understanding that drug trade is, above all, a modern slavery machine that perpetuates the most extreme inequality and massive human suffering, reviving the worst ghosts of history in a contemporary guise.

PART VII: TOWARDS ECONOMIC DE-NARCOTIZATION

The failure of the war on drugs isn't operational; it's paradigmatic. Combating a socioeconomic phenomenon with pure military force and repression is a categorical error. The real "fight" must migrate from the battlefield to the realm of development, justice, and the formal economy. This transition, called economic denarcotization, is not pacifism, but an intelligent strategy to defuse criminal power by attacking its business model and recruitment base.

This work represents a fundamental shift in the diagnosis and approach to the drug trade phenomenon. After thoroughly deconstructing the slave-based and feudal logic of the cartels in the previous chapter, this section definitively abandons the "war" paradigm to propose a comprehensive strategic framework: economic denarcotization. Far from being a simple collection of well-intentioned ideas, this chapter articulates a concrete and multifaceted roadmap that attacks the problem at its structural roots. Its central premise is as lucid as it is compelling: an economic system cannot be fought with bullets; it can only be deactivated by competing with it on its own terrain: the economy and social control.

The analysis is structured around four interconnected pillars, each addressing a specific front of the battle:

1. **The Cultural and Narrative Battle**: Recognizes that the power of narcotics is based on a powerful mythology of success and power. It proposes a counter-narrative of social engineering, based on raw data and real testimonies, to dismantle the narcotic fantasy and reveal the brutal equation of exploitation it truly offers.
2. **The Construction of Real Economic Alternatives**: It transcends welfare and proposes a strategic investment in territorial development. Through rigorous economic calculation, it demonstrates that investing in seed capital, logistics infrastructure, and local value chains is not only more humane, but infinitely more cost-effective than repressive spending on helicopters and operatives.
3. **The Reorientation of Justice:** Proposes a paradigm shift from punitive criminal justice to restorative justice that focuses on victims and the repair of the social fabric. It proposes concrete mechanisms, such as an autonomous reparation fund financed with seized assets, to transform the wealth of crime into an instrument of healing.
4. **The Financial Heart Attack:** This is the most audacious and crucial axis. It accurately identifies that transnational crime's only real vulnerability is its need to launder money. It proposes a "total financial war" that prioritizes financial intelligence, pursues money launderers more viciously than traffickers, and globally attacks the tax havens and digital assets that shield their profits.

Overall, this chapter not only critiques the failure of current policies but also offers a detailed and well-founded manual for action. Its value lies in the coherence with which it interweaves cold-blooded economic analysis with a deep understanding of social harm, proposing a transition from a logic of repression to one of construction.

Economic denarcotization thus emerges not as a soft option, but as the intelligent and necessary strategy to dismantle the criminal power of the 21st century where it truly resides in its economy and its capacity to corrupt and subjugate.

7.1. Demystifying Narco-Success: An Educational and Cultural Counter-Narrative

THE PREVAILING NARRATIVE about drug trade—glorified in ballads, series, and popular stories—is a powerful recruiting tool that sells a fantasy of power, quick riches, and respect. Combating this requires a powerful and multifaceted social engineering approach that goes beyond simply saying "it's wrong" but rather demonstrates, with stark data and powerful stories, that the path of organized crime is a death trap with a losing economic equation. It's about dismantling the myth and revealing the reality of a system of feudal exploitation.

1. Pedagogy of Real Failure: Statistics as a Deterrent Weapon

The strategy must shift from moral admonitions to incontrovertible evidence, using data-driven shock marketing.

- **"Raw Reality" Campaigns (Shock Advertising):**

Content: Develop massive, professionally produced campaigns for social media, community television, and radio. They should use the same visual and audio language as productions that glorify drug trade, but to subvert the message.

Central Message: "Do you know what the real ending is? 99.9% end up dead, maimed, or in a maximum-security prison. Only 0.01% get rich, and you're not them."

Documented Testimonies: Use anonymous testimonies (with silhouettes and voice distortion) from former participants who describe dehumanization, constant paranoia, bloody debts, and post-traumatic stress. Show the true cost: destroyed families, mutilated bodies, ruined lives.

Interactive "Failure Calculator":

Digital Tool: Create an online platform and a simple app where young people can enter their age and background. The tool would calculate, based on real data (life expectancy of a hitman: ~35 years, probability of being incarcerated: ~70%, average salary vs. cartel profit), their concrete probabilities of "success" versus those of dying or being incarcerated. Visualize the overwhelming probability of failure.

2. Financial Risk Education: Revealing the Slave Logic

Transforming the cartel's perverse economic logic into a tangible and repulsive concept, teaching it as a basic survival skill.

- **"The Cartel Economy" Workshops:**

Core Module: "How Much Is Your Life Worth?": Teaching Young People the Cold Equation:

- Annual Maintenance Cost for the cartel (Salary, food, cheap weapon): ~ $15,000 USD.
- Replacement Cost (Recruit and train another): ~ $1,000 USD.

Forged Conclusion: " To the organization, you are 15 times more valuable dead than alive. You are a disposable asset. Investing in your well-being is not a business; replacing you is."

"Risk Wage" Analysis: Teaches how to calculate real hourly income, considering the risk of death or life imprisonment. A salary of $400 USD/month, with a five-year working life expectancy, results in a lifetime income of poverty, in exchange for selling 100% of your future.

3. Cultural Resignification and Creation of New References

It's not enough to destroy the myth; we must build powerful and compelling alternative narratives that uphold legitimate paths.

- **Funding Cultural Counter-Narratives:**

"Corridos de la Resistencia": Support and promote musicians who compose and perform corridos that celebrate the true heroes of the community: the teacher who educates against all odds, the nurse who provides care in the midst of violence, the entrepreneur who opens a factory and creates legitimate jobs, the environmental leader who defends the land.

Cultural Festivals and Competitions: Create massive spaces (in person and online) to honor art, music, film, and literature that tell these new stories of success and resilience.

- **"Mentoring with a Face" Programs:**

Connect at-risk youth with real, accessible role models—local entrepreneurs, engineers, artists, athletes—who have legitimately succeeded in the same context of adversity. They can see, touch, and converse with real success, not illusory ones.

- **Marketing of the Legitimate:**

Develop professional advertising campaigns that position studying, entrepreneurship, and legal employment as acts of rebellion, courage, and true success. Use slogans like: "True power is the power no one can take away from you. Educate it." or "Build your legacy, not your dark side."

Strategic Conclusion: A War of Narratives

The battle against recruitment is, in essence, a war of narratives. The state and civil society must stop ceding this ground and compete with the same force and sophistication with which crime sells its fantasy. This entails:

- Using their own language (visual, musical, popular) to convey an opposite message.
- Arming young people with critical tools (financial education, real data) to make them immune to propaganda.
- Offer seductive and tangible narrative alternatives that satisfy the legitimate desire for recognition, belonging, and social mobility.

Counternarratives are not a complement; they are a strategic frontline in prevention. They aim to unmask the romantic lie to reveal the reality of a system of exploitation that offers crumbs in exchange for a life.

7.2. Real Productive Alternatives: Strategic Investment vs. Repressive Spending

THE PHRASE "LACK OF alternatives" is true, but the solution isn't welfare programs. Integrated territorial economic development policies are needed.

Market-Focused Investment: Instead of subsidies, create seed capital funds, business incubators, and access to soft loans for viable productive projects in high-recruitment areas. For example, with 0.5% of the US 's annual "war" budget ($175 million), 3,500 startups could be created with $50,000 in capital each.

Connectivity and Logistics: The lack of roads and access to markets dooms any agricultural or artisanal project to failure. Investment in basic infrastructure (roads, internet) is a more effective opportunity multiplier than a military battalion.

Local Value Chain: Promote businesses that process raw materials on-site (e.g. , transform coffee or cocoa into high-quality finished products) so that the profit stays in the community and is not exported as a cheap commodity.

The official narrative often repeats that the central problem of drug trade is the "lack of alternatives" for young people and communities in recruitment zones. However, the predominant response has been to launch short-term welfare programs— minimal scholarships, food distribution, and symbolic training—that fail to address the structural roots of the problem. These palliatives do not transform the conditions of exclusion, but rather manage them.

What's needed isn't more "state charity," but rather integrated territorial economic development policies capable of truly competing with the criminal economy by offering horizons of dignity, profitability, and a future.

---

1. Market-Focused Investment

Instead of temporary subsidies, we need to create an ecosystem of productive investment in highly vulnerable areas. Seed capital funds, business incubators, microcredit programs with flexible rates, and mentoring networks can transform communities where today the only option is to join a cartel.

- **Comparative example:** With just 0.5% of the annual budget of the US "war on drugs" (about $175 million), 3,500 community startups could be funded with an initial capital of $50,000 each.
- **While an AR-15 rifle purchased in Texas for $450** can fuel a cycle of violence worth $500,000 in illicit profits, a bakery, a coffee cooperative, or a textile workshop can generate stable employment and community roots.

The challenge is to design viable projects in the market, not mere job simulations.

2. Connectivity and Logistics: Infrastructure as an anti-drug policy

No agricultural, artisanal, or technological project can prosper in communities without passable roads, reliable energy, or internet access. In many of the poppy, marijuana, and coca-producing regions, the cartel is the only player that guarantees logistics: it pays for transportation, purchases inputs, and ensures distribution.

Investing in basic infrastructure—roads, dry ports, digital connectivity, storage systems—is much more effective than deploying a military battalion. Every kilometer of paved road in the mountains not only opens up economic access: it opens up a future alternative that competes with the criminal market.

3. Local Value Chain: Breaking the commodity trap

Farmers who produce coffee, cocoa, avocado, and sugarcane are trapped in the same logic as coca farmers: they sell raw materials at low prices while the added value is concentrated in intermediaries or international markets.

The strategy should be to encourage on-site processing:

- Cooperatives that produce fine chocolate instead of just selling cocoa.
- Roasters that export specialty coffee under a local brand.
- Value-added plants that generate skilled employment in the communities themselves.

In this way, wealth doesn't leak away, but rather circulates within the community, generating economies that are resistant to drug trade.

Critical Synthesis

Current repressive spending fuels the vicious cycle of violence and exclusion: more soldiers, more deaths, more poverty. In contrast, a strategic investment in productive alternatives can create a virtuous cycle where every dollar invested in legal markets, infrastructure, and value chains directly weakens drug trade by diminishing its recruitment power and territorial legitimacy.

Ultimately, the best anti-drug policy is not militarization, but inclusive economic development: transforming the sowing of fear into the sowing of the future.

Comparative impact calculation

Baseline comparison scenario

US "war on drugs" spending, as mentioned earlier). We compare it to two alternative uses:

- **Repressive spending** (military hardware, operation and fumigation)
- **Strategic investment** (seed capital, logistics infrastructure, training and youth employment)

All calculations are conservative and with clear assumptions; where there are ranges, I select the lowest positive impact to avoid overestimating benefits.

Repressive Spending: What $175M Buys

A1) Helicopters + operation

- UH-60/Black Hawk unit cost (base procurement): ~$20–22M
- $175M → 8 helicopters (160–176M) + $15M for initial operation.
- Estimated annual operation: ~$5,000/hr × 400 h/yr × 8 = $16M/yr (fuel, maintenance, crews).
- Typical outcome: Short-term suppression of violence in a given territory, but ballooning (displacement) effect within 12–24 months; 0 cartels sustainably eliminated.
- Cost-effectiveness indicator: $22M per helicopter with no structural effect on recruitment or local economies.

A2) Fumigation (illicit crops)

- Operating cost: ~$6,000/ha (logistics, chemicals, security).
- $175M → 29,166 had sprayed.
- Effect: Replanting in 6–12 months, crop displacement, and social conflict; does not reduce net criminal revenues in the medium term.

A3) Intensive "operations"

- Deployment cost (personnel, per diem, logistics, insurance): difficult to audit; for reference, $175 million covers 3–5 national mega-operations lasting 6–8 weeks.
- Effect: Group fragmentation, violence, and reconfiguration of the criminal landscape; low impact on illicit value chains.
- Synthesis A (repressive): High CAPEX + OPEX, transitory impact, encourages substitution and fragmentation, does not create legal alternatives or reduce the recruitment rate.

B. Strategic Investment: What $175M Yields

- Let's divide the same amount into four complementary levers, which attack the problem through labor supply, logistics, productivity, and settlement.

B1) Seed capital + incubation (real economic competition)

- Allocation: $87.5M (50% of total)
- Model: $50,000 tickets + incubation/mentoring.
- Funded startups/cooperatives: 1,750 (not 3,500, I chose half to be conservative).
- 3-year survival (with incubation): 40% → 700 live businesses.
- Direct employment per unit: 8 positions (micro/small scale).
- Total direct employment sustained: 5,600.
- Average annual income per job: $4,800 (=$400/month).

- Direct annual payroll: $26.9M/year.
- Local multiplier (1.6 conservative): $43.0M/year total economic impact.
- 5-year horizon (no growth, just sustain): $215M aggregate impact.

Note: *If we raise it to 3,500 units (like your example), the results are doubled.*

B2) Logistics infrastructure (rural road + connectivity)

- Allocation: $43.75M (25%)
- Conservative cost: $1M / 10 km (resilient rural roads).
- Work: 437 km.
- Estimated productive impact: 20 productive units per km × +$2,000/year/unit = $40,000/km/year.
- Additional annual income: 437 × $40,000 = $17.5M/year.
- 5-year horizon: $87.6M (excluding new induced investments and tourism).

B3) Local added value (processing at source)

- Allocation: $26.25M (15%)
- Typical projects: coffee roasters, fine chocolate, dairy, agro-processing, textiles.
- Small plants: unit cost $750,000 → 35 plants.
- Direct employment per plant: 25 → 875 direct jobs.
- Additional net annual revenue per plant (conservative): $400,000 (margin capture).
- Total additional annual income: 35 × $400,000 = $14M/year.
- 5-year horizon: $70M.

Key externality: higher local floor price for producers; reduces dependence on intermediaries (and drug trade).

B4) Dual training and first job (cutting the recruitment pipeline)

- Allocation: $17.5M (10%)
- Cost/beneficiary: $1,000 (short training, tutoring, placement).
- Beneficiaries/year: 17,500 young people.
- Effective placement: 40% → 7,000 in formal employment or assisted self-employment.

Social value: reduction of the risk of drug addiction, reduction of homicides and secondary victimization.

Side-by-side comparison (numerical summary)

With $175M:

Repressive (A):

- 8 helicopters + initial OPEX / 29,166 ha fumigated / 3–5 mega operations.
- Structural impact: low; recruitment and routes intact; crime displacement.

Productive (B):

- 1,750 startups (700 sustained for 3 years) → 5,600 direct jobs (tens of thousands indirect).
- 437 km of rural roads → $17.5M/year of additional productive value.
- 35 value-added plants → $14M/year of retained local margin.
- 17,500 young people trained/year → 7,000 placed (recruitment cut-off).

Aggregate annual economic impact (minimum): \$43.0M + \$17.5M + \$14.0M = \$74.5M/year

5-year impact (no growth): \$372.5M—doubles the initial investment and reconfigures local incentives.

If you apply chain-specific multipliers (e.g., specialty coffee, rural tourism, agribusiness), these numbers increase non-linearly.

Cost-effectiveness indicators

Cost per direct job created (B1+B3):

- \$87.5M / 5,600 ≈ \$15,600 for direct employment (with incubation and assets).
- Very competitive against light industrial employment benchmarks .

Cost per enabled km (B2):

- \$100,000/km, with \$40,000/km/year of added value → paybacks ≈ 2.5 years.

Cost per young person placed (B4):

- \$17.5M / 7,000 = \$2,500 per effective insertion (training + placement).

"Cost per homicide avoided" (social proxy):

Although complex, insertion + employment programs tend to be orders of magnitude more cost-effective than militarization (which typically exceeds \$100,000–\$300,000 per "avoided event" in forensic estimates).

Sensitivity (what happens if things turn out worse than expected)

- Third-year business survival rate drops to 30% (down from 40%) → 525 units, 4,200 jobs → Annual payroll ~$20.2M; total impact ~$32.3M/year; still socially profitable.
- Local multiplier drops to 1.3 (from 1.6) → annual impact drops ~19%; paybacks are extended by 6–12 months, but the economics remain.
- Infrastructure with delays → the value is deferred, not destroyed; the project continues to enable the market for 10–20 years.

Conclusion of the comparative calculation

- Repressive spending burns capital on assets with high operating costs and low social returns; it doesn't reduce the recruiting base or create alternatives.
- Strategic investment generates jobs, local roots, and local value chains, with paybacks of 2–5 years and a compounding effect as the business network grows.
- Over 5 years, $175 million directed toward development could multiply its direct economic impact by two to three times and deactivate the incentives that fuel drug trade.

Key message: Every dollar spent today on helicopters or fumigation could buy a future: decent jobs, functional logistics, and local added value. That's anti-drug policy that works.

7.3. Restorative Justice: Victims at the Center of State Policy

THE TRADITIONAL CRIMINAL justice system, focused on capturing and punishing the perpetrator, has proven profoundly inadequate in the context of narco-cultural violence. This model, in addition to its low conviction rate, completely ignores the needs of victims and devastated communities for comprehensive reparations, leaving a void of pain and impunity that fuels cycles of revenge and chronic distrust of the state. It is imperative to reverse this logic, placing reparation and the reconstruction of the social fabric at the center of any justice strategy.

1. Transformative Economic Reparation: From Seized Assets to Community Reconstruction

Justice must have a tangible, material component that demonstrates the State's capacity to restore what the crime took. This requires a swift, transparent, and direct mechanism.

Creation of an Autonomous "National Reparation Fund":

Priority Financing: By law, 100% of assets seized from criminal organizations (money, property, vehicles, businesses) must be automatically allocated to this fund. This turns the wealth derived from crime into an instrument of reparation, both symbolically and materially.

Direct Distribution Mechanism: The fund should operate with minimal bureaucracy and clear criteria. Financial reparations should be direct and timely for families of:

- **Victims of enforced disappearance:** To cover search, therapy, and support costs.
- **Forced displacement:** For relocation, housing and economic recovery.
- **Survivors of massacres and extreme violence:** For medical and psychological care and life projects.

Investment in Collective Productive Projects: A portion of the fund must be allocated to community reparations: the construction of schools, health centers, parks, or productive infrastructure in the most affected communities. Thus, reparations are not only individual but collective, healing the public spaces damaged by violence.

2. Local Truth and Reconciliation Processes: Justice as Healing, not just Punishment

Beyond the courts, we need community spaces that confront historical truth and build the foundation for future peace.

Local Hearings of Truth:

Objective: To create safe spaces, facilitated by trusted civil society organizations and state institutions, where victims can narrate their pain and receive public recognition, and where perpetrators (who have opted for a transitional justice route) can contribute to the truth in exchange for limited penal benefits.

Result: These processes do not seek to replace criminal justice, but rather to complement it. Their goal is to build a shared truth that dismantles the distorted narratives of criminal power, dignifies victims, and lays the foundation for future coexistence. It is an antidote to forgetting and denial.

Reconciliation and Non-Repetition Programs:

Focus: Develop concrete programs in schools and communities that, based on recognized truth, work on:

- Preventing the stigmatization of families of victims or ex-combatants.
- The construction of a historical memory that honors the victims and alerts future generations to the horrors of violence.
- The creation of community pacts for peace and legality.

3. Procedural Justice and Real Access: Specialized Courts and Comprehensive Support

Restorative justice requires a strengthened institutional framework that is accessible to victims.

Specialized Units for the Search for Missing Persons:

Provide technical and budgetary autonomy to search units, with interdisciplinary teams (forensics, anthropologists, psychologists) working closely with family groups. The truth about the whereabouts of a loved one is a fundamental form of reparation.

Specialized Courts with a Victims' Perspective:

Create special chambers within the judicial system to handle organized crime offenses, with trained judges, robust witness protection programs, and psychosocial support teams for victims who must testify. The judicial process itself should not be a source of secondary victimization.

Conclusion: From a Justice that Punishes to one that Reconstructs

The restorative justice paradigm proposes a radical shift: understanding that crime is not only an offense against the state, but a profound harm against specific individuals and communities. Therefore, the measure of judicial success should not be solely the number of incarcerated people, but the number of lives repaired, communities stabilized, and cycles of violence broken.

Implementing this model is a declaration that the State values the lives of its citizens more than revenge against their perpetrators. It is the basis for rebuilding the legitimacy of the State and demonstrating, with actions, that there is a dignified, and effective institutional path to healing the nation's deepest wounds. True security is not born from more weapons, but from more justice.

7.4. Redesigning the Fight: The Economic Dismantling of Crime

THE FUNDAMENTAL FLAW of the "war on drugs" has been its tactical myopia: focusing on the weakest and most replaceable link in the chain—the foot soldier and the cocaine shipment—while leaving the true heart of the business untouched: money. As the DEA demonstrated in 2010, 99% of the cocaine intercepted worldwide was replaced in less than six months, while the laundered money remained unreachable in top-tier banks. In other words: every kilo seized was replaced, every laundered dollar remained safe.

The 21st century demands a radical strategic shift. Transnational organized crime's only real vulnerability is its imperative to integrate trillions of blood-stained dollars into the global financial system. Without this conversion, money is dead paper. With it, it is transformed into political power, social influence, and military capability. Attacking this network is the only way to break the backbone of drug trade.

1. Total Financial War: "Follow the Money" as a guiding principle

The new paradigm must abandon the mirage that capturing drug lords or spraying hectares of land are strategic victories. A kilo of cocaine seized is a media success; a laundering network dismantled is a historic victory.

Massive strengthening of financial intelligence

- **Triple resources:** Units like the UIF in Mexico or the UIAF in Colombia must transform from bureaucratic offices into full-fledged financial intelligence agencies, with the same status as a counterterrorism agency. This means tripling their budgets, recruiting hybrid profiles (forensic economists, blockchain experts, data engineers), and equipping them with artificial intelligence capable of tracking invisible patterns in massive transaction volumes.
- **Specialized prosecutors:** Judges and prosecutors trained exclusively in complex financial crimes are needed. The average criminal lawyer is ill-equipped to dismantle a scheme

involving 30 shell companies, crypto accounts, and offshore trusts in the Virgin Islands. Without specialists, cases collapse in court.

Asymmetric criminal incentives: Money laundering should be punished more severely than drug trade. The message: trafficking is replaceable; laundering is unforgivable. The launderer prolongs the business and protects it; without him, the entire system collapses.

2. Systemic attack on money laundering mechanisms

Drugs travel in tons; money, in computer clicks. Organized crime cannot survive without a global infrastructure of complicity comprised of bankers, lawyers, notaries, and tax havens.

Offensive against tax havens and shell companies

- **Diplomatic pressure and sanctions:** The G20 and the FATF must stop issuing symbolic gray lists and move on to real sanctions. A country that protects banking secrecy is not a "tax haven": it is a criminal sanctuary. It must receive economic sanctions equivalent to those imposed on states that finance terrorism.
- **Public registry of beneficial owners:** Today, millions of properties and businesses are registered in the name of front men or opaque corporations. A public, verifiable, and mandatory registry of beneficial owners would be a nuclear bomb against the invisibility of drug trade, equivalent to exposing to the sun an organism that only survives in the dark.

Aggressive regulation of digital assets

Training and tools: Cartels already operate with cryptocurrencies, NFTs, and mixers. Continuing to track suitcases of banknotes is as obsolete as searching for fax messages. Agency teams need to be equipped with blockchain software. forensics, specialized equipment and legal powers to freeze digital assets in real time.

Collaboration with global exchanges: Just as the banking system was forced to apply KYC (Know Your Customer), cryptocurrency exchanges must comply with equivalent protocols. Without effective regulation, they become the new Swiss banking system of the 21st century.

3. Reorientation of international cooperation: from helicopters to auditors

International cooperation programs have failed because they have funded military hardware that strengthens both the state and the drug cartels infiltrated within it. Plan Mérida and Plan Colombia invested billions in helicopters, rifles, and radars that ended up integrated into the criminal infrastructure.

The new model must migrate from the military to the financial and technical.

- **Change of priorities:** Cooperation resources should be allocated to civilian financial intelligence units, not to fumigation or patrol battalions.
- **Teams of international specialists:** Instead of sending troops, send forensic auditors, cryptocurrency experts, and anti-corruption prosecutors. Each team should work alongside local authorities in real-life asset tracing and freezing cases.
- **Legal Harmonization:** Today, a drug trafficker can lose property in Colombia but legally transfer it to Panama or Dubai. Without international harmonization of asset forfeiture laws, the system will remain a Gruyère cheese of global impunity.

Conclusion of the great strategic shift

Economic denarcotization is not a complementary policy; it's the only viable strategy to address the root of the problem. It means abandoning the obsession with rifles and hectares and concentrating all state power on the true center of gravity: the flow of illicit capital.

From bullets to balance sheets: Instead of spending billions on bullets that multiply violence, invest in financial intelligence that dismantles the business.

Competing for the future: It's not enough to suffocate capital; it's about offering real alternatives, where credit, decent employment, or a local business are more attractive than the false promise of drug-related wealth.

Winning the war that matters: The battlefield is no longer in the mountains of Sinaloa or the jungles of Colombia: it's in the law firms of Miami, the property registries of Dubai, and the servers processing crypto transactions in Singapore.

Drug traffickers don't die when a boss falls; they die when money stops circulating. The real war isn't against cocaine: it's against the bank balance sheets that give it life.

Narco Money Explosion: From Bills to Global Chaos

Center of the Explosion:

$1 of drug origin

First Ring (immediate impact):

- **Direct bribery:** police officers, judges and military personnel are bought.
- **Gun Purchase:** An AK-47 for $450 in Texas → $5,000 in Mexico.
- **Recruitment:** A hawk child earns $50 a week, caught in the cycle of violence.

Second Ring (structural impact):

- **Bank laundering:** 99.8% of drug money makes its way into the global financial system without consequences.

- **Real estate investment:** skyscrapers in Miami, Monterrey, or Panama City, empty but "profitable."
- **Cryptocurrencies and tax havens**: guaranteed anonymity on a digital scale.

Third Ring (social and political impact):

- Institutional corruption: prosecutors, governors, and presidents financed by drug money.
- State vacuums: communities where drug trade replaces the government as the de facto authority.
- Multiplied violence: cartel fragmentation, local wars, and mass displacement.

Fourth Ring (global impact):

- **International complicity:** banks in Switzerland, Dubai, and London legitimizing capital.
- **Inflated market:** Ban generates a +500% overprice, multiplying profits by 16 times.
- **Irreversible human damage:** entire generations subjected to fear, trauma and dependence on criminal economies.

The result of the explosion: Every drug dollar multiplies like a shock wave that ripples through bodies, cities, banks, and governments. The system doesn't collapse by accident: it's designed so that the explosion never stops, feeding off itself with each new injection of illicit capital.

STRUCTURAL ANALYSIS TOWARDS ECONOMIC DE-NARCOTIZATION

The "war on drugs" has failed because it attacked with bullets what was essentially an economic and social problem. As long as drug trade remains the most profitable option in impoverished territories, no operation can compete against the logic of survival. The real alternative lies not in more patrols or more prisons, but in defunding crime by creating legal opportunities that are equally profitable and sustainable.

1. Effective alternatives in affected territories

The case of Medellín is illustrative. Agroecology and rural development programs (Mayor's Office, 2023) have shown that offering legal options not only generates income but also reduces youth recruitment by 45%. These projects do not consist of simple subsidies, but rather entire ecosystems: access to land, technical training, product marketing, and community support. The result is that the local economy no longer depends on drug trade, but rather on a sustainable productive framework that strengthens the social fabric and breaks the cycle of violence.

2. Responsibility and global learning

The Portuguese model of decriminalization and harm reduction is a global lesson: investing in public health, education, and prevention reduced drug-related deaths by up to 90% in two decades. Portugal demonstrated that repression does not eliminate consumption or trafficking, but it does increase violence and deaths. By shifting the logic of persecution to one of social integration, the country turned the problem into a health challenge, not a battlefield. The message is clear: dollars invested in bullets fail; those invested in prevention save lives.

3. Impactful testimonies: life in the face of violence

The numbers become more vivid when you hear the voices of those who managed to escape the drug trade. A former drug lord who participated in job reintegration programs recounted:

"Now I grow legal coffee... I earn the same as I do as a falcon, but I live."

(Young People Building the Future Program)

This testimony summarizes the core of drug control: legitimate economic competition can replace the criminal incentive. When legality pays the same—and also offers security, dignity, and a future—the promise of drug trade loses its appeal.

4. Structural conclusion: from repression to resilience

Economic denarcotization is not an abstract ideal, but a concrete strategy that requires three axes:

- **Generating competitive legal income:** jobs, cooperatives, and value chains that compete profitably with the drug industry.
- **Investment in education, health, and community:** not as a healthcare expenditure, but as a preventative infrastructure that reduces the breeding ground for recruitment.
- **Reducing the cartels' economic power:** not just through confiscations, but through smart regulation and productive alternatives that challenge their monopoly.

In short, prevention is cheaper than repression, but it's also fairer, more humane, and more effective. This approach transforms prevention into resilience and opens the door for abandoning drug trade to cease being a death sentence and become a dignified, viable, and sustainable option.

Final Analysis: Economic Denarcotization as a Strategic Imperative

TOWARD ECONOMIC DENARCOTIZATION is not just a propositional chapter; it is the cornerstone of the entire previous structural analysis. It represents the logical bridge between the devastating critique of the cartels' slavery model—developed in this final chapter—and the construction of a viable solution paradigm. Its value lies in the fact that it transcends denunciation to present a comprehensive, multifaceted strategic framework grounded in an economic and social logic as robust as that employed by organized crime itself.

This final analysis seeks to synthesize the key contributions of this chapter, assess its internal coherence and viability, and highlight the paradigm shift it proposes for security and development policy.

1. From Failed War to Strategic Competition: A Paradigm Shift

The chapter begins with an unquestionable diagnosis: the failure of the war on drugs is paradigmatic, not operational. For decades, the strategy was based on a categorical error: combating a socioeconomic phenomenon (the supply of employment and income in contexts of exclusion) with pure military force (the demand for eradication and capture). This approach has not only been useless—as evidenced by the rates of violence and the constant flow of drugs—but has also been counterproductive. Militarized repression has fragmented cartels, multiplied violence, corrupted institutions, and, most seriously, consolidated criminal territorial control by eliminating any semblance of the rule of law in vast regions.

Faced with this scenario, the proposal for economic denarcotization constitutes a Copernican shift. It is no longer about "winning a war," but about disabling a business model and competing for the loyalty of the population. The enemy is not an army to be defeated, but an economic logic of exploitation to be dismantled. This shift in mentality is the chapter's first and most crucial contribution.

2. The Four Pillars of a Comprehensive Strategy: Coherence and Depth

The strength of the proposal lies in its multidimensionality. It recognizes that there is no silver bullet and, therefore, articulates four simultaneous and synergistic fronts of action:

a) The Battle for the Narrative (Cultural Demystification): This chapter understands that drug trade is, to a large extent, a system of symbolic power. Ballads, series, and the narrative of "narco-success" are recruiting tools as powerful as money. The proposal for an " educational and cultural counternarrative " is brilliant because it doesn't limit itself to moral sermons. Instead, it proposes using the enemy's own weapons—shock marketing, powerful visual language, raw testimonies—to reveal the reality: drug trade is a feudal system where 99.9% end up dead, imprisoned, or traumatized, and only a tiny elite becomes rich. The "Failure Calculator" and the "Pedagogy of Real Failure" are concrete and applicable ideas that aim to immunize the most vulnerable population—young people—through economic rationality and truthful testimony.

b) The Construction of Real Alternatives (Productive Investment): This is the central economic pillar and the clearest demonstration of the proposal's viability. The chapter overcomes the vagueness of "creating jobs" and offers a strategic investment plan quantitatively compared to repressive spending. The calculation is revealing: the same $175 million spent on helicopters and fumigation operations—with zero or negative impact—can finance a productive ecosystem of 1,750 community startups, 437 km of rural roads, and 35 value-added plants, generating thousands of stable jobs and an annual wage bill of tens of millions of dollars.

The key here is the market approach. We are not proposing welfare subsidies, but rather investment in viable projects, with incubation, mentoring, and connection to value chains. We are attacking the root cause of recruitment: the lack of legitimate economic options that compete in profitability and dignity with the criminal market.

c) Reparation as Justice (Restorative Justice): This pillar introduces an ethical and historical dimension absent from security policies. It proposes a shift from a criminal justice system obsessed with punishment—which often revictimizes and leaves social harm untouched—to a restorative justice system that centers victims and the community.

The creation of an autonomous National Reparations Fund, financed with 100% of assets seized from crimes, is a powerful idea both symbolically and materially. It transforms the instruments of oppression (criminal wealth) into tools of healing. Complemented by local truth and reconciliation processes, this approach seeks to rebuild the social fabric devastated by violence, which is a prerequisite for any form of sustainable peace.

d) The Attack on the Nervous Center (Financial Warfare): This is possibly the chapter's most strategic and modern contribution. It accurately identifies that the true vulnerability of transnational crime lies not in the poppy fields or the hitmen, but in their imperative need to launder trillions of dollars.

The proposal for a "total financial war" is a guidebook for the 21st century. It proposes:

- Triple the resources of financial intelligence units.
- Pursue money launderers more viciously than traffickers.
- Attack tax havens with real sanctions.
- Aggressively regulate cryptocurrencies and require exchanges to implement anti-corruption protocols.
- Reorient international helicopter cooperation toward forensic auditors and financial specialists.

This approach recognizes that the battlefield is no longer the mountains, but the global financial system. A cartel without money laundering capabilities is a cartel doomed to suffocation.

---

3. Feasibility and Challenges: A Complex but Necessary Path

The proposal is robust, but its implementation faces monumental obstacles:

Political Will: It demands a long-term vision of the state that transcends electoral cycles and confronts powerful vested interests, both within the (corrupt) state apparatus and in international banking.

International Coordination: Financial warfare requires unprecedented coordination between countries to harmonize asset forfeiture laws and sanction tax havens, something that conflicts with geopolitics and national sovereignty.

Institutional Capacity: Building the technical capacity for financial intelligence and restorative justice requires time, resources, and profound reform of the judicial and security systems.

Despite these challenges, the chapter demonstrates that the current path is unsustainable and far more costly. Economic denarcotization is not the "soft" option; it's the smart option. Investing in development is, as calculations show, more cost-effective than spending on repression.

Conclusion: Towards a Post-Narco Future

This final chapter culminates the central argument of the entire work: drug trade is an economic and political system of exploitation, not a simple criminal problem. Therefore, its solution cannot be police-based, but rather civilizing. Economic denarcotization is the framework for building this alternative. It is a strategy that understands that we must compete on all fronts: in the cultural narrative, in the economic offering, in the administration of justice, and in the financial system. It offers no magic bullets, but rather a rigorous, coherent, and deeply hopeful work plan.

Its final message is clear: true victory against drug trade is not measured by captured kingpins or tons of drugs seized, but by stable communities, young people with a future, and an economy where blood money can no longer be laundered. That's the only war worth fighting, and this chapter provides the roadmap for winning it.

EPILOGUE

Throughout this book, I have tried to be reasonable, even-handed, and, above all, proactive. My intention was not to remain in futile denunciation, but rather to seek viable solutions to a phenomenon that devours lives, institutions, and entire generations. However, upon rereading what I have written, I recognize that there is something impossible to hide: the anger and rage that comes from seeing how drug trade has become a deadly epidemic, spreading throughout the world like a virus that respects no borders or social classes. What we are seeing is no longer a local or even regional problem: it is a challenge that has gotten out of hand for all of humanity. New laws and old prohibitionist prescriptions are not enough. Anti-drug programs designed to sugarcoat statistics are not enough. And even less so are more guns, more bullets, and more corpses. If we have learned anything in more than half a century of the "war on drugs," it is that repeating conventional formulas only multiplies failure. Therefore, the challenge demands breaking paradigms and contemplating the unthinkable.

Drug trafficking is a real monster, but not a mythological one. It doesn't live in dark caves, but in our streets, in our government institutions, and in the banking system. It is a global system that confronts us with the worst of ourselves. And that is why its solution will not come from a single law, a single president, or a military strategy. The true solution demands a different civilizational pact, a shift that challenges economic, political, and cultural interests on a global scale.

This book does not claim to have all the answers. Rather, it seeks to open up the questions that concern us all. Because the problem is no longer just drug trade: the problem is humanity's entire problem. And as long as we continue to manage the disaster instead of transforming it, the only certain thing is that the bill will continue to be paid in the most expensive currency of all: human lives.

I'll begin by saying what, in my opinion, went wrong from the very beginning with drug use and regulation. And perhaps I should go back not just a few decades, but two centuries, to the opium dens in England or the Opium Wars that pitted Imperial China against the British Empire. Back then, it was already clear that the problem wasn't the substance itself, but the way states and markets turned it into an instrument of domination, plunder, and profit. At this point, searching for a single culprit is as absurd as trying to figure out who discovered fire. The history of drugs has no clear beginning or lone villain; it is the history of humanity coexisting with substances that relieve pain, expand consciousness, or enslave bodies, always depending on the social, political, and economic context in which they are used. What we can say with certainty is that, from those first "errors" of management and prohibition, humanity sowed the seeds of a global catastrophe: turning a public health problem into a problem of military repression and a gold mine for organized crime.

Today we are reaping the consequences. What began as a tolerated market in opium dens, a trade that enriched colonial powers, ended up degenerating into a transnational industry of pain, moving hundreds of billions of dollars annually and feeding on the blood of the poorest. Prohibition, rather than containing the phenomenon, made it exponentially profitable. And the violence we experience today is nothing more than an echo of that original error.

First point. I am convinced that drug use and drug addiction, serious and painful problems, should never have become a national crusade or an issue of international security. Use is, above all, an individual and family phenomenon, with an immediate impact on those close to us: parents, siblings, partners, friends. However, what should have been treated as a public health problem became a collective monster, where the fundamental error was turning the decision—or misfortune—of some into the problem of all.

Because it's undeniable: human beings have a self-destructive drive, and drugs are one of the most obvious vehicles of that fragility. But the fact that someone decides—out of desperation, pleasure, or ignorance—to consume a substance shouldn't be equivalent to mortgaging the fate of an entire country. When the State turns drug addiction into a national war, the spiral of costs becomes absurd: multi-million-dollar budgets bleed into failed strategies.

If the government is right-wing, the prescription is usually the same: more guns, more bullets, more helicopters, more armored vehicles. If the government is left-wing, the remedy changes its name, but not its substance: poorly designed social programs, created with good intentions, end up functioning as enormous black holes through which millions of dollars of public funds are lost without addressing the root of the problem. In both cases, the pattern repeats itself: drug traffickers win, the population loses, and the state is wasted.

What's being overlooked is that the real battle was never about whether to buy rifles or distribute scholarships, but about recognizing that individual consumption shouldn't have become a collective cause of militarization and massive corruption. The personal tragedy of drug addiction ended up becoming a national tragedy, not because it was inevitable, but because the institutions made the wrong decision from the start. And that mistake dragged us all into a problem that today seems to have no solution.

Second point. The great mistake of many governments has been to treat addicts with caution, as if they were untouchable. We oscillate between two equally ineffective extremes: criminalizing them as dangerous criminals or overprotecting them as if they were eternal victims with no responsibility for their actions. Both positions are wrong.

The solution is another: to recognize that as long as addicts don't harm others, they shouldn't be imprisoned or prosecuted. However, they can't continue to be shielded by excessive legal safeguards that force families, schools, or businesses to endure behaviors that destroy entire environments. Society can't be condemned to forever bear the burden of someone who chose to use drugs and who, furthermore, insists on normalizing their use at everyone's expense.

Current laws are so permissive as to be absurd. Human Rights has descended into a misguided paternalism: it forces employers to keep workers on the payroll who arrive high on drugs, prevents schools from expelling students who use drugs in the classroom, and, in many cases, leaves families defenseless, no longer knowing how to protect themselves from an addicted son, brother, or husband. This is unsustainable.

The proposal is clear: responsibility must return to the individual. If a family grows tired and wants to file a restraining order against a violent or destructive addict, they should be able to do so without hindrance. If a company administers a drug test and detects drug use, it should have the right to fire the person, always with transparency mechanisms to prevent abuse, but without the absurd obligation to keep someone unproductive or risky on the payroll. And in the case of schools, if a student uses drugs, the institution should have the power to expel them to protect the rest of the student community.

This doesn't mean denying second chances. On the contrary: a recovered addict who demonstrates with actions—not just words—that he or she has left substance use behind deserves to fully reintegrate without stigma. Because no one is perfect, and recovery is possible. But in the meantime, the line must be drawn: society is under no obligation to adapt to anyone's drug addiction.

In short: the message must be clear. Those who choose to use drugs will find doors closed at work, at school, and in their family life. Not as an irrational punishment, but as a logical consequence. And those who manage to escape this cycle will find those same doors open again. Only in this way can we break the vicious cycle of victimization and permissiveness that has made the addict not only a personal problem, but an unfair collective burden.

Third point. Having only one perspective on drug use and trafficking is as dangerous as having none at all. Repeating this is not a lack of consistency, but an act of intellectual honesty: this problem has no single correct answer, nor can it be solved by passing a couple of laws or moralizing rhetoric. To pretend otherwise is naive or, worse, willful blindness. Therefore, although it may sound contradictory to what I've said before, here I advocate a proposal that goes in a different direction: the creation of authorized consumption zones. Specifically demarcated places regulated by the State where any adult over 18 can consume drugs under strict conditions. Why? Because it's necessary to separate private, controlled consumption from the uncontrolled public consumption we see today on the streets, in schools, in parks, even in front of children.

The rule must be clear and unequivocal: consumption may only be carried out within these authorized areas. Doing so outside these areas would have severe consequences, ranging from 18 months of arrest to harsher administrative sanctions, such as the obligation to report the incident to future employers. It may sound extreme, but if the message is not clear, consumers will continue to believe that permissiveness is unlimited and that any space can become a place for unpunished consumption.

This system must not be thrown into the void, as some European countries did, legalizing or tolerating consumption without ever questioning the source of these drugs, as if they arose spontaneously. It's not enough to open "consumption rooms" while the black market remains intact and the cartels continue to supply them.

Therefore, this proposal must be accompanied by complementary measures: in authorized areas, not only should consumption be allowed, but also the limited production of certain low-impact drugs (such as marijuana, peyote, and hallucinogenic mushrooms) must be regulated to ensure that what circulates in these spaces does not come from criminal organizations, but from crops supervised and controlled by the State or authorized communities.

In this way, two problems are attacked simultaneously:

Consumption is restricted and controlled to specific spaces, reducing the social impact and the risk of normalization in children and adolescents.

- The black market is beginning to be dismantled, taking away part of the production and distribution monopoly from drug traffickers.
- If we accept that drug use will never disappear, the most rational thing to do is not to continue denying reality, but to design a system where drug use is no longer linked to violence, crime, and bloodshed.

In this sense, I propose a radical but logical model: regulated barter conventions and conditional production permits for hard drugs (heroin, cocaine, amphetamines). The principle is simple: if a citizen wants to produce drugs for personal use or for exchange in authorized spaces, the State should grant them a permit with one unbreakable condition: what is manufactured cannot be sold on the black market or used for business. Its purpose must be exclusively recreational, in a closed circuit between producers and consumers who mutually recognize each other as "responsible users."

This may sound utopian, but in reality, it's not so different from what happens with craft beer or those who produce their own wine. In this model, drugs cease to be a product of war and become a cultural, recreational, or ritual product, without the need to kill or die for them. If the rules are followed, self-managed drug communities could even emerge, removed from the criminal circuit, where the freedom to use drugs doesn't imply the condemnation of dragging an entire country into the hell of violence.

Now, this doesn't contradict what was said in the second point: being free to consume in authorized spaces doesn't mean others are obligated to tolerate you. An addict who breaks the rules by consuming in unauthorized places or harming others must face clear sanctions. But if someone respects the limits, doesn't attack anyone, and stays within the legal framework, there's no reason to prosecute them. Furthermore, being a declared addict doesn't necessarily turn someone into a pariah. Many companies, in practice, already know that some of their employees use drugs. What matters to them isn't the employee's private life, but rather that they stick to their schedule, deliver results, and maintain their performance. The same thing happens in social relationships: many friends don't care whether one uses marijuana, cocaine, or LSD; what really matters to them is that the person doesn't lose control or sink into the inability to pay for their consumption.

In short, this point raises a fundamental premise: the problem isn't the drug itself, but the structural violence its prohibition produces. If we eliminate the black market through a regulated system of production and consumption—where the state merely enforces compliance—then much of the cartels' reason for existence disappears. And with that, the country could begin to break out of the vicious cycle of bloodshed and corruption that prohibition has cemented for decades.

In conclusion, this third point doesn't negate the previous ones: it complements them. Because confronting drug crisis requires thinking from multiple angles and breaking paradigms. Neither total repression nor absolute permissiveness are solutions; we need a middle path, strict in its regulation, but realistic in its application. The "authorized zones" option isn't perfect, but it can be a turning point in taming what is today an out-of-control beast.

Fourth Point. Drug trafficking as a tyrannical regime: the urgency of extraordinary measures

I've repeatedly emphasized throughout this analysis that the drug trade problem cannot be solved with one or two laws, well-intentioned social programs, or by sending more weapons and soldiers into the streets. And I repeat it here because this insistence isn't a defect: it's a necessity. Drug cartels are no longer simple criminal gangs; they have become de facto tyrannical regimes, capable of controlling territories, dictating the rules of life and death, and subjugating entire populations through fear. They are as dangerous as any dictatorship that has marked the history of humanity with blood.

Faced with this, conventional responses are insufficient. Diplomatically, the correct course of action would be to demand that drug trade leaders be brought before international courts and tried for crimes against humanity, because that is what they are: executioners who have enslaved entire peoples under a system of terror. However, I must also recognize that such a scenario could end up being a reward, a legal spectacle that grants them status and notoriety, as has happened with other war criminals.

Therefore, I maintain that the solution is not to negotiate or make deals with them, because agreements with the cartels are worthless: they work in the short term, but they always end up consolidating their power. The only way to root out this terror regime is to make them pay a real, tangible, and non-negotiable price. And here I must be brutally honest: these leaders and their collaborators must be eliminated without hesitation. They must be hanged with barbed wire, preferably a damned rusty wire.

I'm not just talking about the visible bosses, but also their inner circles: the front men, the financial operators, and yes, even the family members who have directly and knowingly benefited from the collective suffering. Because drug trade isn't just an armed army: it's a parasitic network that feeds on everyone's wealth, and as long as there are pockets of family and economic impunity, there will always be room for it to resurface.

Is this drastic? Yes. Is it repetitive? Yes. But I reiterate once again, because this is not a flippant opinion: as long as drug trade has nothing to lose, nothing will change. Their logic is based on the fact that they are always allowed to negotiate, flee, or retrain. History confirms this: when they fall, their money, their heirs, or their partners continue to drive the wheels.

That's why this point is doubly important:

- I must reiterate that the problem is beyond the reach of conventional solutions.
- I want to emphasize that there will be no peace as long as the cartels can continue to accumulate power without facing real existential losses.

In short: drug trade is not negotiated with; it is defeated or endured. And defeating it requires a level of toughness and moral clarity that humanity, until now, has been unwilling to embrace.

Fifth Point: Technology, Money, and the End of Simulation: The Battle of the Future

I've insisted throughout this book that the "war on drugs" can no longer be reduced to the exchange of bullets in the streets. That strategy has proven to be a vicious cycle: more weapons, more clashes, more deaths, but zero structural results. If anything needs to change fundamentally, it's the very way it's fought. And the key isn't rifles or patrols, but technology and tracking capital. Because the truth is simple: money doesn't disappear. The billions raised by the cartels flow through accounts, real estate, front men, and tax havens. Ignoring that route and continuing to focus on cocaine or armored trucks is like chasing shadows while leaving the monster's power source intact.

This is where the United States and other countries have an enormous responsibility. If they truly want to "help" Mexico and the region, they shouldn't send helicopters or advisors patrolling like they did during the Cold War. That's an archaic strategy, typical of a bygone century. Real help consists of transferring financial tracking technology, artificial intelligence, and satellite surveillance to monitor in real time money routes, criminal operation zones, and logistics warehouses where weapons and drugs are hidden.

Today, there are tools capable of identifying suspicious transactions on blockchain , cross-referencing international banking databases, and detecting patterns that reveal illicit operations. There is the potential to use autonomous drones to map entire regions, and algorithms that predict criminal mobility with minimal margins of error. The future is here, but we continue to fight with the weapons of the past.

Of course, technology isn't enough: political will is also needed. And in this sense, it's hypocritical for the US to fund anti-drug programs while simultaneously negotiating, making deals, or protecting drug lords who are useful to it in certain contexts. This double standard not only undermines any strategy but also perpetuates the criminal cycle. If international cooperation is to make sense, it must begin by breaking these pacts of convenience.

And as for the fate of the big bosses, I'll say it bluntly: the death penalty should be applied in an exemplary manner. Not because they seek revenge, but because the supposed "negotiations" or "information" they provide upon arrest have never served to dismantle an entire cartel. What they hand over is low-value data, crumbs to entertain the system, but never the financial core or the networks of political complicity. It's junk information. The real information is in their accounts, their bank transactions, and property records.

Therefore, this point ends with a clear conviction:

- **More intelligence**, fewer bullets.
- **More algorithms,** fewer helicopters.
- **More financial tracking,** less aimless patrols.

The battle of the future will not be won by randomly shooting young, disposable hitmen, but by stifling the flow of capital that keeps the criminal system alive. And if governments aren't willing to use this technology head-on, all they'll do is prolong this endless war that's already devouring entire generations.

General Conclusion

In conclusion, this is a problem of enormous complexity that will not be solved simply or immediately. And it will be even less resolved if there is no political and social will to address its true roots: corruption, dirty money, and indifference to collective suffering. The war on drugs is not lost for lack of weapons, but for lack of courage to break the hidden pacts that sustain it.

As long as there is no real decision—not rhetoric or pretense—to use available technology, root out criminal financing, and adopt comprehensive policies that put life before business, the problem will continue to grow like an uncontrolled epidemic.

What this book demonstrates is that bullets aren't enough, nor are isolated social programs enough, nor is it enough to blame the consumer or the producer. What's required is a multifaceted, courageous, and disruptive strategy capable of breaking traditional paradigms.

The ultimate question is not whether we can end drug trade, but whether we are willing to pay the price to confront it seriously: abandon hypocrisy, make radical decisions, and accept that great changes are never born from fear or comfort, but from conviction.

A Reasonable Doubt

Is the Sinaloa Cartel's $14 billion annual or cumulative?

1. The short answer

Yes, these are annual profits. It's an approximate cash flow that the DEA calculated at the height of the Sinaloa Cartel's reign under Joaquín "El Chapo" Guzmán (2017). It's not the accumulated wealth of his entire career, but rather the amount the criminal organization generated in a single year.

---

2. The $14 billion as annual flow (gross income)

Source: Estimates presented during Guzmán's trial in New York (2019), based on DEA investigations.

What it means: Total value of drugs moved wholesale in one year.

It is not net profit: Operating costs (bribes, transportation, salaries, weapons, logistics) must be subtracted from this volume.

Comparative dimension: The Sinaloa Cartel generated more revenue than legal corporations such as:

- **Netflix in 2017:** ~11.7 billion USD
- **Mattel in 2017:** ~4.9 billion USD
- **Twitter in 2017:** ~2.5 billion USD

---

3. Accumulated assets (stock)

El Chapo Guzmán: Forbes listed him in 2009 with an estimated personal fortune of ~$1 billion, although other estimates put the figure at between $12 and $14 billion.

Key difference:

- $14 billion a year = cartel's annual revenue (flow).
- $12–14 billion in total = Guzmán's personal wealth accumulated over decades of criminal career (stock).

---

4. Critical interpretation

Cash flow isn't the same as fortune: The $14 billion wasn't in Guzmán's single bank account but rather represents the entire organization's annual capital turnover.

Distribution of the money: The bosses keep a fraction of the cash flow (5–10%). This equates to between $500 million and $1.4 billion annually in the hands of the top brass.

Money on the loose: A significant portion is lost in bribery, money laundering, violence, and logistics.

---

5. Conclusion

The $ 14 billion figure should be read as follows:

- It is the annual income of the organization at its peak of operations.
- It is not equivalent to the personal wealth of a drug lord, although his accumulated assets may come close in total.
- In business terms, it's like talking about the "annual sales" of a criminal multinational.
- What's truly alarming isn't just the economic magnitude, but the internal inequality: while the top brass accumulates billions, 99.9% of cartel members die in poverty and extreme violence.

Additional Data and Final Questions

To truly grasp the corrosive power of this business, we must talk about numbers. Drug trafficking is estimated to generate global revenues exceeding $500 billion annually, a figure that rivals the GDP of entire countries and makes it one of the most lucrative markets on the planet. This flow of capital fuels corruption, finances violence, and buys impunity on an industrial scale.

However, this sea of money raises two uncomfortable and essential questions that undermine the official narrative:

1. The Unusual Disparity of the Fortunes Seized:

It doesn't seem feasible that, over the course of a lifetime of crime, the so-called "bosses" of cartels accumulate personal fortunes that, while obscene to an ordinary citizen, pale in comparison to the brutal revenues of the business they control. If their income is so colossal, and their operating expenses—despite being based on a slave labor force—are significant in logistics, weapons, and bribes, where is all the money? A fortune calculated for a magnate of this caliber should be measured in hundreds of billions of dollars, not mere billions. That agencies like the FBI or the DEA report seized fortunes of "14 billion" for a kingpin of the stature of Joaquín "El Chapo" Guzmán seems laughable. It's as if the assets of Jeff Bezos or Elon Musk magically evaporate every year. This abysmal discrepancy gives rise to disturbing speculation: could these official figures be rigged? The possibility that corrupt public officials systematically enrich themselves every time they capture a drug lord—understating the true loot in reports and diverting the rest—would explain the opacity and obsession with capturing high-profile targets, often preceded by opaque negotiations. It's a speculative theory, but no one can deny that the math doesn't add up, and the distrust is more than justified.

2. Facades or Real Owners?

The other possibility, perhaps more terrifying, is that the men presented as the absolute lords of drug trade are merely the visible faces of a much deeper and more powerful structure. If the seized fortunes are so relatively "small," perhaps it is because these bosses were never the true owners of the business, but rather operational managers whose ultimate destiny was prison or death to protect the true beneficiaries. This would imply that the millions of dollars in profits end up in the accounts of an invisible elite—bankers, businessmen, politicians—who remain in the shadows, immune and untainted, laundering their money in the global licit economy while the "bosses" serve as scapegoats in an eternal cycle of violence that very conveniently diverts attention from them.

In conclusion, the question isn't just how to stop the violence, but who's actually keeping the money? Until the financial flow is audited and pursued with the same ferocity as the hitman or the grower, any "victory" will remain an mirage, or worse, part of the business.

Glossary of Acronyms and Abbreviations

---

1. **ATF (Bureau of Alcohol, Tobacco, Firearms and Explosives):** The United States Bureau of Alcohol, Tobacco, Firearms and Explosives. It is the federal agency responsible for investigating firearms-related crimes.
2. **IDB (Inter-American Development Bank):** International financial institution that supports economic and social development projects in Latin America and the Caribbean.
3. **CDMX:** Abbreviation for Mexico City.
4. **ECLAC (Economic Commission for Latin America and the Caribbean):** United Nations agency that promotes economic and social development in the region.
5. **CIDAC (Center for Development Research, AC):** A think tank Mexican tank focused on the study of public policies.
6. **CIDE (Center for Economic Research and Teaching):** Mexican institution of higher education and research in social sciences.
7. **IACHR (Inter-American Commission on Human Rights):** Body of the Organization of American States (OAS) dedicated to the promotion and protection of human rights.
8. **CJNG (Jalisco New Generation Cartel):** One of Mexico's largest and most violent transnational criminal organizations.
9. **Colmex (El Colegio de México):** Prestigious Mexican institution of research and higher education in social sciences and humanities.
10. **CONEVAL (National Council for the Evaluation of Social Development Policy):** Mexican agency responsible for measuring poverty and evaluating government social programs.
11. **DEA (Drug Enforcement Administration):** United States

Drug Enforcement Administration. It is the federal agency responsible for combating drug trade.

12. **DW (Deutsche Welle):** Germany's international broadcasting service.
13. **FATF (Financial Action Task Force):** In Spanish, FATF. It is an intergovernmental body that establishes standards to combat money laundering.
14. **FBI (Federal Bureau of Investigation):** Federal Bureau of Investigation. It is the principal criminal investigation agency of the United States government.
15. **FLACSO (Latin American Faculty of Social Sciences):** International organization dedicated to research and teaching in the field of social sciences.
16. **FNA (National Anti-Drug Force):** Honduran entity responsible for combating drug trade.
17. **FATF (Financial Action Task Force):** Spanish version of FATF.
18. **GAO (Government Accountability Office:** The United States Government Accountability Office. It is the investigative agency of Congress.
19. **IMCO (Mexican Institute for Competitiveness):** A Mexican research center that generates analysis of economic phenomena for the improvement of public policies.
20. **INEGI (National Institute of Statistics and Geography):** Autonomous agency of the Mexican government responsible for national censuses and official statistics.
21. **LLC (Limited Limited Liability Company:** A type of business structure in the U.S. that can be used to conceal the identity of the beneficial owner.
22. **MSMEs:** Acronym for Micro, Small and Medium Enterprises.
23. **MOE (Electoral Observation Mission):** Colombian

organization that monitors electoral processes and the relationship between politics and armed actors.

24. **MS-13 (Mara Salvatrucha):** A transnational criminal gang with a strong presence in Central America and the United States.
25. **MXN:** Symbol of the Mexican Peso.
26. **NFT (Non-Fungible Token):** A unique digital asset, referred to in the text as a sophisticated method for money laundering.
27. **IOM (International Organization for Migration):** United Nations agency working in the field of migration.
28. **ILO (International Labour Organization):** United Nations agency dealing with matters related to labour and industrial relations.
29. **UNODC (United Nations Office on Drugs and Crime):** Spanish version of UNODC.
30. **PAHO (Pan American Health Organization):** International public health organization dedicated to improving health in the Americas.
31. **GDP (Gross Domestic Product):** Economic indicator that represents the total value of goods and services produced in a country.
32. **PJF (Federal Judicial Branch):** Body of the Mexican government responsible for administering justice at the federal level.
33. **UNDP (United Nations Development Programme):** UN agency that promotes development and combats poverty.
34. **ROI (Return on Investment):** Return on Investment. A financial metric that evaluates the profitability of an investment compared to its cost.
35. **Sedena (Secretariat of National Defense):** Ministry of Defense of Mexico, in charge of the Army and the Air Force.
36. **PTSD (Post-Traumatic Stress Disorder):** A mental health

condition triggered by experiencing or witnessing a terrifying event.

37. **UAM (Metropolitan Autonomous University):** One of the main public universities in Mexico.
38. **UCA (Central American University "José Simeón Cañas"):** Jesuit university located in El Salvador.
39. **EU:** Abbreviation for the European Union.
40. **UIF (Financial Intelligence Unit):** Mexican government agency responsible for preventing and combating money laundering.
41. **UIAF (Financial Information and Analysis Unit):** Colombian government agency with functions similar to the UIF of Mexico.
42. **UNAM (National Autonomous University of Mexico):** The largest and most important public university in Mexico.
43. **UNICEF (United Nations International Children's Emergency Fund):** United Nations Children's Fund.
44. **UNODC (United Nations Office on Drugs and Crime):** United Nations Office on Drugs and Crime.
45. **USD:** Symbol for the United States Dollar.

Also by Mikel Sandór Piña

Der Zolldämon
Tolddæmonen
De Tarief Demon
El Demonio de los Aranceles
LE DÉMON DES TARIFS
TARIFFDEMONEN
TARIFFDEMONEN
Tariffidemoni
The Tariff Demon
Vamos Tarde
Vamos Atrasar
We're Late
Esclavos del Narco
Slaves of the Cartels

www.ingramcontent.com/pod-product-compliance
Lightning Source LLC
LaVergne TN
LVHW090322210926
848480LV00001B/328